ISBN 978-1-4400-9154-4
PIBN 10003240

This book is a reproduction of an important historical work. Forgotten Books uses state-of-the-art technology to digitally reconstruct the work, preserving the original format whilst repairing imperfections present in the aged copy. In rare cases, an imperfection in the original, such as a blemish or missing page, may be replicated in our edition. We do, however, repair the vast majority of imperfections successfully; any imperfections that remain are intentionally left to preserve the state of such historical works.

1 MONTH OF
FREE
READING

at
www.ForgottenBooks.com

By purchasing this book you are eligible for one month membership to ForgottenBooks.com, giving you unlimited access to our entire collection of over 700,000 titles via our web site and mobile apps.

To claim your free month visit:
www.forgottenbooks.com/free3240

English
Français
Deutsche
Italiano
Español
Português

www.forgottenbooks.com

Mythology Photography **Fiction**
Fishing Christianity **Art** Cooking
Essays Buddhism Freemasonry
Medicine **Biology** Music **Ancient
Egypt** Evolution Carpentry Physics
Dance Geology **Mathematics** Fitness
Shakespeare **Folklore** Yoga Marketing
Confidence Immortality Biographies
Poetry **Psychology** Witchcraft
Electronics Chemistry History **Law**
Accounting **Philosophy** Anthropology
Alchemy Drama Quantum Mechanics
Atheism Sexual Health **Ancient History**
Entrepreneurship Languages Sport
Paleontology Needlework Islam
Metaphysics Investment Archaeology
Parenting Statistics Criminology
Motivational

WOODCRAFT SERIES

CAMP-LORE AND WOODCRAFT

FOURTH IMPRESSION

WOODCRAFT SERIES

THE AMERICAN BOYS' HANDYBOOK OF CAMP-LORE AND WOODCRAFT

BY

DAN BEARD

FOUNDER OF THE FIRST BOY SCOUTS SOCIETY; AUTHOR OF "THE AMERICAN BOYS' BOOK OF SIGNS, SIGNALS AND SYMBOLS," ETC.

WITH 577 ILLUSTRATIONS BY THE AUTHOR

PHILADELPHIA AND LONDON
J. B. LIPPINCOTT COMPANY

D217932

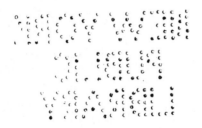

TO

GEORGE DU PONT PRATT

COMMISSIONER OF CONSERVATION, STATE OF NEW YORK
SCOUT, SPORTSMAN AND OUTDOOR MAN

FOREWORD TO THE SECOND EDITION

Boys, if this foreword is too "highbrow" for your taste, skip it, but the author don't believe you will, and even if he has used some dictionary words he feels that you will forgive him after he tells you that he did so only because of the lack of time to think up more simple terms. What he wants to say is that . . .

Boyhood is a wonderful and invaluable asset to the nation, for in the breast of every boy there is a divine spark, materialists call it the "urge of youth," others call it the "Christ in man," the Quakers call it the "inner light," but all view it with interest and anxiety, the ignorant with fear and the wise with understanding sympathy, but also with a feeling akin to awe.

Those of us who think we know boys, feel that this "inner light" illuminating their wonderful powers of imagination, is the compelling force culminating in the vigorous aecomplishments of manhood. It is the force which sent Columbus voyaging over the unknown seas, which sent Captain Cook on his voyage around the world, the same force which carried Lindbergh in his frail airship across the Atlantic. Yes, it is the sublime force which has inspired physicians and laymen to cheerfully risk and sacrifice their lives in search of the cause of Yellow Fever, Anthrax, Hydrophobia and other communicable diseases . . . no, *not* for science but for

HUMANITY!

FOREWORD TO THE SECOND EDITION

As a boy, the author dreamed of wonderful municipal playgrounds, of organizations giving the boys opportunity to camp in the open, of zoological and botanical gardens planned and adapted to the understanding of youth. His busy life as a civil engineer, surveyor, and work in the open gave him no opportunity to develop his dreams, but at the end of a five year tour of the United States and Canada, made over fifty years ago, he drifted into New York City and was shocked beyond expression by the almost total lack of breathing spaces for our boys, in the greatest of American cities. True, it then had Central Park; but fifty years ago Central Park was out among the goats, only to be reached by a long and tiresome horse car journey.

This lamentable state of affairs caused the writer so much real pain and concern that he then and there inaugurated a personal crusade for the benefit of the boys, a crusade with the avowed object of winning for them the peoples' interest in the big outdoors.

The most difficult part of his task was to convince the men of the swivel chairs that boys' leisure should be spent in the open; that the blue sky is the only proper roof for a normal boy's playground; also that the open spaces are the places where God intended young people to live, work and play.

No great crusade, no great movement of any kind is one man's work, nevertheless, every successful movement must have *one enthusiast* in the front rank, one who knows the trail and comprehensively envisions the objective—*objectum quad complexum*. Others may and will join him, and occasionally spurt ahead of the leader, like the hare in the fable, but the enthusiast keeps right on just the same.

Pray do not understand by this that the writer claims

that he alone is responsible for this bloodless revolution. No, no, his propaganda work did however win for him the moral support of the editorial staff of *St. Nicholas*, *Youth's Companion* and *Harpers*. Later he was openly backed and encouraged by such distinguished sportsmen as President Roosevelt, his chief forester Governor Pinchot, and his Chief of Staff Major General Bell. While the stalwart men of the Camp Fire Club of America worked hand and glove with him, all similar organizations failed not in voicing their approval. Furthermore he was always helped by his loyal friends of the daily press. Many famous writers lent their influence, all working consciously or unconsciously to help the great cause of boyhood.

The author only claims that, in all these fifty long years, he has never ceased to work for the boys, never wavered in his purpose, and now?—well, when he marched at the head of fifty thousand Scouts in the great muddy outdoor Scout camp at Birkenhead, England, he realized that his ephemeral air castles had settled down to a firm foundation upon Mother Earth.

Yes, boys we have won a great victory for *boyhood*! We have won it by iteration and reiteration, in other words, by shouting *outdoors*, talking *outdoors*, picturing *outdoors*, singing *outdoors* and above all by writing about the *outdoors*, and constantly hammering on one subject and keeping one purpose always in view. By such means we have at last, not only interested the people of the United States in the open, but stampeded the whole world to the forests and the fields. So let us all join in singing the old Methodist hymn:—

FOREWORD TO THE SECOND EDITION

"Shout, shout, we are gaining ground,
Glory, Hallelujah!
The Devil's kingdom we'll put down,
Glory, Hallelujah!"

The Devil's kingdom in this case is the ill-ventilated
school rooms, offices and courts.

It is well to note that the work in this book was not done
in the library, but either in the open itself or from notes and
sketches made in the open. When telling how to build a
cooking fire, for instance, the author preferred to make his
diagrams from the fires built by himself or by his wilderness
friends, than to trust to information derived from some other
man's books. It is much easier to make pictures of impractical fires than to build them. The paste pot and scissors
occupy no place of honor in our woodcraft series.

So, Boys of the Open, throw aside your new rackets, your
croquet mallets, and your boiled shirts—pull on your buckskin leggings, give a war whoop and be what God intended
you should be; healthy wholesome boys. This great Republic belongs to you and so does this

BOOK OF CAMP-LORE AND WOODCRAFT.

DAN BEARD

Suffern, New York,
December first,
1930.

FOREWORD

HIDDEN in a drawer in the antique highboy, back of the moose head in my studio, there are specimens of Indian bead work, bits of buckskin, necklaces made of the teeth of animals, a stone calumet, my old hunting knife with its rawhide sheath and—carefully folded in oiled paper—is the jerked tenderloin of a grizzly bear!

But that is not all; for more important still is a mysterious wooden flask containing the castor or the scentgland of a beaver, which is carefully rolled up in a bit of buckskin embroidered with mystic Indian signs.

The flask was given to me as "big medicine" by Bow-arrow, the Chief of the Montinais Indians. Bow-arrow said—and I believe him—that when one inhales the odor of the castor from this medicine flask one's soul and body are then and forever afterwards permeated with a great and abiding love of the big outdoors. Also, when one eats of the mystic grizzly bear's flesh, one's body acquires the strength and courage of this great animal.

During the initiation of the members of a Spartan band of my boys, known as the Buckskin Men, each candidate is given a thin slice of the grizzly bear meat and a whiff of the beaver castor.

Of course, we know that people with unromantic and unimaginative minds will call this sentimentalism. We people of the outdoor tribes plead guilty to being sentimentalists; but we *know* from experience that old Bow-arrow was right, because we have ourselves eaten of the grizzly bear and smelled the castor of the beaver!

While the writer cannot give each of his readers a taste of this coveted bear meat in material form, or a whiff of the beaver medicine, direct from the wooden flask made by the late Bow-arrow's own hands, still the author hopes that the magical qualities of this great medicine will enter into and form a part of the subject matter of this book, and through that medium inoculate the souls and bodies of his readers, purify them and rejuvenate them with a love of the WORLD AS GOD MADE IT.

DAN BEARD

June, 1920

CONTENTS

vii

CHAPTER I

FIRE MAKING BY FRICTION

HOW TO MAKE A FIRE-BOARD, BOW, DRILL AND THIMBLE

INDIAN LEGEND OF THE SOURCE OF FIRE

RECORD FIRE-MAKERS

RUBBING-STICK OUTFIT

ESKIMO THIMBLE

BOW, BOW-STRING, THIMBLE, FIRE-BOARD, FIRE-PAN

TINDER, CHARRED RAGS, PUFF BALLS

FIRE-MAKERS OF THE BALKAN

FIRE WITHOUT A BOW, CO-LI-LI, THE FIRE SAW

FIRE PUMPING OF THE IROQUOIS

PYROPNEUMATIC APPARATUS

CAMP-LORE AND WOODCRAFT

CHAPTER I

FIRE MAKING BY FRICTION

WHEN THE "what-is-its" of Pithecantropus erectus age and other like hob-goblin men were moping around the rough sketch of an earth, there were no camp-fires; the only fire that these creatures knew was that which struck terror to their hearts when it was vomited forth from volcanic craters, or came crashing among them in the form of lightning. No wonder that the primitive men looked upon fire as a deity, no doubt an evil deity at first but one who later became good.

When the vast fields of ice covered Europe during the glacier period and forced men to think or die, necessity developed a prehistoric Edison among the Neanderthal men, who discovered how to build and control a fire, thus saving his race from being frozen in the ice and kept on cold storage, like the hairy rhinoceros and elephant of Siberia.

The fire of this forgotten and unknown glacier savage was the forerunner of our steam-heaters and kitchen ranges; in fact, without it we could have made no progress whatever, for not only the humble kitchen range, but the great factories and power-plants are all depending upon the discovery made by the shivering, teeth-chattering savage who was hopping around and trying to keep himself warm among the European glaciers.

But we people of the camp-fires are more interested in primitive fires just as the Neanderthal men built them, than

3

we are in the roaring furnaces of the steel works, the volcano blast furnaces, or any of the scientific, commercialized fires of factory and commerce.

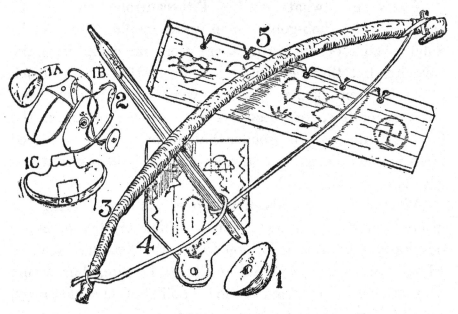

What we love is the genial, old-fashioned camp-fire in the open, on the broad prairie, on the mountainside, or in the dark and mysterious forests, where, as our good friend Dr. Hornaday says,

> We will pile on pine and spruce,
> Mesquite roots and sagebrush loose,
> Dead bamboo and smelly teak,
> And with fagots blazing bright
> Burn a hole into the night—

Not long ago the author was up North in the unmapped lake country of Canada, and while camping on the portage between two wild and lonely lakes, Scout Joe Van Vleck made himself a fire outfit consisting of Fig. 1, a thimble made of a burl, with which to hold Fig. 2, the spindle made of balsam. Fig. 3 is a bow cut from a standing bush; not an elastic bow, such as one uses with which to shoot arrows, but a bow with a permanent bend to it. Fig. 4 is the fire-pan which is placed under the fire-board to catch the charcoal dust as it falls through the slot when the spindle is twirled.

Fig. 5 is the fire-board, made of a dead balsam tree which was standing within three yards of the camp-fire.

In order to make his fire it was necessary for our Scout to have some tinder, and this he secured from the bark of cedar trees, also within a few yards of our camp. This indeed was a novel experience, for seldom is material so convenient. The fire was built in a few seconds, much to the wonderment of our Indian guide, and the delight of some moose hunters who chanced to be crossing the portage on which our camp was located.

It was an American, Dr. Walter Hough of the U. S. National Museum of Washington, who first proved that a modern up-to-date civilized white man can make a fire with rubbing-sticks, as well as the primitive man. But it was an Englishman who popularized this method of making fire, introduced it among the Boy Scouts of England and America, and the sister organizations among the girls.

According to the American Indian legend the animal people who inhabited the earth before the Redmen lived in darkness in California. There was the coyote man, the vulture man, the white-footed mouse man, and a lot of other fabled creatures. Away over East somewhere there was light because the sun was over there, and the humming-bird man among the animal people of our Indians is the one, according to Dr. Merriman, who stole the fire from the East and carried it under his chin. The mark of it is still there. The next time you see a humming-bird note the brilliant spot of red fire under his chin.

Now you understand why the king-pin in fire mak-ing at your camp deserves the title of Le-ché-ché (the humming-bird).

If one gets the fire from a fire-board, spindle and bow in record time, then the title of Le-ché-ché is all the more appro-priate because it was the humming-bird man who hid the fire in the oo-noo tree, and to this day, when the Indian wants fire, he goes to the oo-noo (buckeye) tree to get it; that is, provided he has no matches in the pockets of his store clothes and that some white boy, like the Scout previously mentioned, has taught him how to make fire as did the Indian's own ancestors. But even then the oo-noo* wood must be dead and dry.

Austin Norton of Ypsilanti, Michigan, April, 1912, made fire in thirty-nine and one-fifth seconds; Frederick C. Reed of Washington, in December, 1912, made fire in thirty-one sec-onds; Mr. Ernest Miller of St. Paul made fire in thirty sec-onds, but it was Mr. Arthur Forbush, one of the author's Scouts of the Sons of Daniel Boone (the scout organization which preceded both the English Boy Scouts and the Boy Scouts of America) who broke the record time in making fire with "rubbing-sticks" by doing it in twenty-nine seconds at the Sportsman's Show at Madison Square Garden, New York. Mr. Forbush made this record in the presence of the author and many witnesses. Since then the same gentleman reduced his own world-record to twenty-six and one-fifth seconds ; by this time even that record † may have been broken.

The "rubbing-stick" is a picturesque, sensational and

* It is not the buckeye of the Ohio and Mississippi Valley, but is the nut buckeye of California, Æsculus Californica.

† The record is now eleven seconds.

interesting method of building a fire, but to-day it is of little practical use outside of the fact that it teaches one to over-come obstacles, to do things with the tools at hand, to think and act with the vigor, precision and self-confidence of a primitive man.

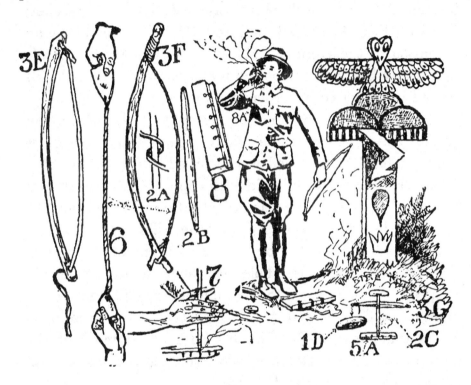

"Rubbing-stick" Outfit

Ever since the writer was a small boy he has read about making fire by rubbing "two chips" or "two sticks" together, and he was under the impression then, and is under the impression now, that no one can build a fire in that manner. When we find reference to rubbing-sticks it is probably a slovenly manner of describing the bow and drill and the other similar friction fire implements. For the bow and drill one requires first a

Thimble

(Figs. 1, 1A, 1B, 1C and 1D). This is a half round stone
or pebble, a half round burl or knot of wood, or it may be
made of soft wood with an inlay of a piece of stone. In the
bottom of the thimble there is always a shallow hole or socket;
see S on Figs. 1, 1A, 1B, 1C, and 1D. The thimble is an
invention of the Eskimos (Fig. 1C); they keep the spindle
upright by holding the pointed upper end of it in a hole (S)
drilled into a piece of serpentine, or soapstone.

The author has a thimble personally made for him by
Major David Abercrombie. This beautiful implement is
made of hard fine-grained wood carved into the form of a
beetle (Fig. 1B). It is inlaid with copper and semi-precious
stones. The socket hole was drilled into a piece of jade (B),
using for the purpose some sand and the drill shown in Fig. 23.
There was a piece of steel pipe set into the end of the wooden
drill with which to bore a hole into the hard jade. The jade
was then inlaid or set into the middle of the bottom of the
thimble, and cemented there, Fig. 1B. The author also
has a thimble made for him by Edmund Seymour of the
Camp-fire Club of America. This thimble is a stone fossil
with a hole drilled in it, Fig. 1A.

It is not necessary to tell the reader that when using the
bow for power, the twirling spindle cannot be held down with
the bare hand, consequently the use of the thimble for that
purpose is necessary. Fig. 1C shows an Eskimo thimble so
fashioned that it may be held in the fire-maker's mouth.

The Bow

Is a stick or branch of wood (Figs. 3, 3E, 3F and 3G) about
a foot and a half long and almost an inch in diameter, which

has a permanent bend in it—the bend may be natural or **may** have been made artificially. To the bow is attached a slack thong, or durable string of some kind. The Eskimos, more inventive than the Indians, made themselves beautiful bows of ivory, carving them from walrus tusks, which they shaved down and strung with a loose strip of walrus hide.

THE BOW STRING

The objection to whang string or belt lacing is that it is apt to be too greasy, so if one can secure a strip of buckskin, a buckskin thong about two inches wide, and twist it into a string, it will probably best serve the purpose (Fig. 6).

THE SPINDLE

The spindle is the twirling stick (Figs. 2, 2A, 2B and 2C) which is usually about a foot long and was used by our American Indians without the bow (Fig. 7). The twirling stick or spindle may be three-quarters of an inch in diameter at the middle; constant use and sharpening will gradually shorten the spindle. When it becomes too short a new one must be made. The end of the spindle should not be made sharp like a lead pencil, but should have a dull or rounded end, with which to bore into the fire-board, thus producing fine, hot charcoal, which in time becomes a spark: that is, a growing ember.

THE FIRE-BOARD

The fire-board (Figs. 5 and 5A) should be made of spruce, cedar, balsam, tamarack, cottonwood root, basswood, and even dry white pine, maple and, probably, buckeye wood. It should not be made of black walnut, oak or chestnut, or any wood which has a gummy or resinous quality. The fire-board should be of dry material which will powder easily. Dr. Hough recommends maple for the fire-board, or "hearth," as it is called in the Boy Scout Handbook. Make the fire-board about eleven inches long, two inches wide and three-quarters of an inch thick.

Near the edge of the board, and two inches from the end, begin a row of notches each three-quarter inch long and cut down through the fire-board so as to be wider at the bottom. At the inside end of each notch make an indenture only sufficiently deep to barely hold the end of your spindle while you make the preliminary twirls which gradually enlarge the socket to fit the end of your spindle.

THE FIRE-PAN

The fire-pan is a chip, shingle or wooden dust-pan used to catch the charred dust as it is pushed out by the twirling spindle (Fig. 4). The use of the fire-pan is also an Eskimos idea, but they cut a step in their driftwood fire-board itself (Fig. 8) to serve as a fire-pan.

TINDER

When you can procure them, charred rags of cotton or linen make excellent tinder, but the best fabric for that purpose is an old Turkish towel.

HOW TO CHAR A RAG

Find a flat stone (Fig. 10), a broad piece of board, a smooth, hard, bare piece of earth; set your cloth afire and after it begins to blaze briskly, smother it out quickly by using a folded piece of paper (Fig. 9), a square section of birch bark or another piece of board. This flapped down quickly upon the flames will extinguish them without disturbing the charred portion (Fig. 10). Or with your feet quickly trample out the flames. Keep your punk or tinder in a water-tight box; a tin tobacco box is good for that purpose, or do like our ancestors did—keep it in a punk horn (Fig. 30).

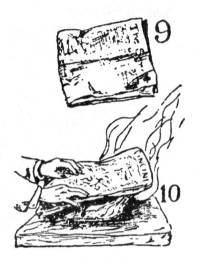

Very fine dry grass is good tinder, also the mushroom, known as the puff-ball or Devil's snuff-box. The puff-balls, big ones, may be found growing about the edges of the woods and they make very good punk or tinder. They are prepared by hanging them on a string and drying them out, after which they are cut into thin slices, laid on the board and beaten until all the black dust ("snuff") is hammered out of them, when they are in condition to use as punk or tinder (Fig. 11). In olden times there was a mushroom, toadstool or fungus imported from Germany, and used as punk, but woodcraft consists in supplying oneself with the material at hand; therefore do not forget that flying squirrels (Figs. 12 and 13), white-footed mice (Fig. 14) and voles, or short-tailed meadow mice, are all addicted to collecting good

TINDER

with which to make their warm nests: So also do some of the birds—the summer yellow bird, humming-bird and vireos. While abandoned humming-birds' nests are too difficult to find, last year's vireos' nests are more easily discovered suspended like cups between two branches, usually within reach of the hand, and quite conspicuous in the fall when the leaves are off the trees.

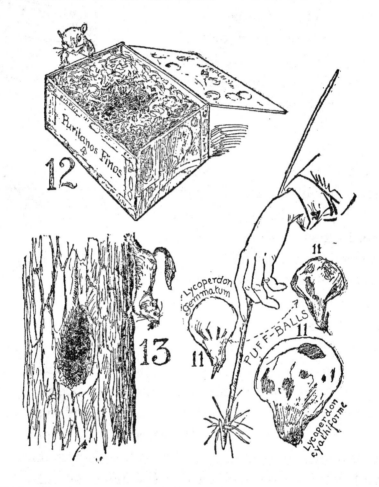

Cedar bark, both red (Fig. 15) and white, the dry inner bark of other trees, dry birch bark, when shredded up very fine, make good tinder. Whether you use the various forms of rubbing-sticks or the flint and steel, it is necessary to catch the spark in punk or tinder in order to develop the flame.

How to Make a Fire with a Drill and Bow

First find a level solid foundation on which to place your fire-board, then make a half turn with the string of the bow around the spindle, as in the diagram (Fig. 16); now grasp the thimble with the left hand, put one end of the drill in the socket hole of the thimble, the other end in the socket hole on the fire-board, with your left foot holding the fire-board down.

Press your left wrist firmly against your left shin. Begin work by drawing the bow slowly and horizontally back and

forth until it works easily, work the bow as one does a fiddle bow when playing on a bass viol, but draw the bow its whole length each time. When it is running smoothly, speed it up.

Or when you feel that the drill is biting the wood, press harder on the thimble, not too hard, but hard enough to hold the drill firmly, so that it will not slip out of the socket but will continue to bite the wood until the "sawdust" begins to appear. At first it will show a brown color, later it will become black and begin to smoke until the thickening smoke

announces that you have developed the spark. At this stage
you gently fan the smoking embers with one hand. If you
fan it too briskly, as often happens, the powder will be
blown away.

As soon as you are satisfied that you have secured a spark,
lift the powdered embers on the fire-pan and place carefully
on top of it a bunch of tinder, then blow till it bursts into
flame (Fig. 8A). Or fold the tinder over the spark gently,
take it up in your hand and swing it with a circular motion
until the flame flares out.

Even to this day peasantry throughout the Carpathian
and Balkan peninsulas build their fires with a "rubbing-
stick." But these people not being campers have a permanent fire machine made by erecting two posts, one to represent
the fire-stick and the other the socket thimble. The spindle
runs horizontally between these two posts and the pressure
is secured by a thong or cord tied around the two posts, which
tends to pull them toward each other. The spindle is worked
by a bow the same as the one already described and the fire
is produced in the same manner.

Fire Without a Bow

My pupils in the Woodcraft Camp built fires successfully by using the rung of a chair for the spindle, a piece of packing case for a fire-board, and another piece for the socket wood and the string from their moccasins for a bow string. They used no bow, however, and two or three boys were necessary to make a fire, one to hold the spindle and two others to saw on the moccasin string (Fig. 17).

Co-li-li—the Fire Saw

is made of two pieces of bamboo, or fish pole. This is the oldest instrument for fire making used by the Bontoc Igorot and is now seldom found among the men of the Philippines. Practically all Philippine boys, however, know how to make and use it and so should our boys here, and men, too. It is called "co-li-li" and is made of two pieces of dry bamboo. A two-foot section of dead and dry bamboo is first split lengthwise and in one piece, a small area of the stringy tissue lining of the tube is splintered and picked until quite loose (Fig. 18). Just over the picked fibres, but on the outside of the bamboo, a narrow groove is cut across it (Fig. 18G). This piece of bamboo is now the stationary lower part or "fire-board" of the machine.   One edge of the other half of the original tube is sharpened like a chisel blade's edge (Fig. 19); it is then grasped with one hand at each end and is slowly and heavily sawed backward and forward through the groove in the board, and afterwards worked more rapidly, thus producing a conical pile of dry dust on the wad of tinder picked from the inside of the bamboo or previously placed there. (Figs. 20 and 21).   Fig. 22 is the fire-pan.

"After a dozen strokes," says our authority, Mr. Albert Ernest Jenks, "the sides of the groove and the edge of the piece are burned down; presently a smell of smoke is plain and before three dozen strokes have been made, smoke may be seen.   Usually before a hundred strokes a larger volume of smoke tells us that the dry dust constantly falling on the pile has grown more and more charred until finally a tiny spark falls, carrying combustion to the already heated dust cone."

The fire-board is then carefully lifted and if the pinch of dust is smouldering it may now be gently fanned with the hand until the tinder catches; then it may be blown into a flame.

Fire Pumping of the Iroquois

Fig. 23 shows another form of drill.   For this one it is necessary to have a weight wheel attached to the lower part of the spindle.   A hole is made through its center and the drill fitted to this.   The one in Fig. 23 is fitted out with a rusty iron wheel which I found under the barn.   Fig. 23 C shows a pottery weight wheel which I found many years ago in a gravel-pit in Mills Creek bottoms at Cincinnati, Ohio.   It was brick-red in color and decorated

with strange characters. For many, many years I did not
know for what use this unique instrument was intended. I
presented it to the Flushing High School (Long Island), where
I trust it still remains. The fire-drill is twirled by moving
the bow up and down instead of backward and forward.

THE TWIRLING STICK (American Indian)

Fig. 7 is practically the same as Figs. 16 and 17, with this
difference: the bow and thong are dispensed with and the
spindle twirled between the palm of the hands, as formerly
practised by the California Indians, the natives of Australia,
Caroline Islands, China, Africa and India.

Many of the American Indians made friction fire in this
manner. They spun the thin spindle by rolling it between
the palms of their hands and as pressure was exerted the
hands gradually slid down to the thick lower end of the
spindle. To again get the hands to the top of the drill requires
practice and skill. Personally the writer cannot claim any
success with this method.

THE PLOW STICK (American Indian)

The simplest method of friction is that of the plow, which
requires only a fire-board with a
gutter in it and a rubbing-stick
to push up and down the gutter
(Fig. 24). Captain Belmore
Browne of Mt. McKinley fame
made a fire by this last method
when his matches were soaked
with water. It is, however, more
difficult to produce the fire this
way than with the thong and

bow. It is still used in the Malay Islands; the natives place the fire-board on a stump or stone, straddle it and with a pointed drill plow the board back and forth until they produce fire. Time: Forty seconds.

Of course it is unnecessary to tell anyone that he can start a fire with a sunglass (Fig. 25) or with the lens of a  camera, or with the lens made from two old-fashioned watch crystals held together. But as the sun is not always visible, as lenses are not supposed to grow in the wild woods and were not to be found in the camps and log cabins of the pioneers, and as watch crystals have short lives in the woods, we will pass this method of fire making without matches as one which properly belongs in the classroom.

The Pyropneumatic Apparatus

Before or about the time of the American Revolution some gentleman invented a fire piston (Fig. 26) with which he ignited punk made of fungus by the heat engendered by the sudden compression of the air.

The ancient gentleman describes his invention as follows: "The cylinder is about nine inches long, and half an inch in diameter; it terminates in a screw on which screws the magazine intended to hold a bougie, and some fungus. A steel rod is attached to a solid piston, or plunger, not shown in the figure, it being within the tube. This rod has a milled head and there is a small hole in the tube to admit the air, when the piston is drawn up to the top, where a piece unscrews, for the purpose of applying oil or grease to the piston. I have found lard to answer the end best."

Method of Using It

" Take from the magazine a small piece of fungus, and place it in the chamber, screw the piece tight on and draw the piston up by the end, till it stops. Hold the instrument with both hands in the manner represented in Fig. 26, place the end on a table or against any firm body, either in a perpendicular, horizontal or vertical direction, and force the piston down with as much rapidity as possible. This rapid compression of the air will cause the fungus to take fire. Instantly after the stroke of the piston, unscrew the magazine, when the air will rush in, and keep up the combustion till the fungus is consumed. Observe, in lighting the tinder, the

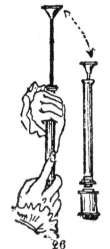

fungus must be lifted up a little from the chamber, so as to allow the tinder to be introduced beneath it, otherwise it will not kindle.

"Here it may be remarked that the instrument thus constructed has a decided advantage over the fire-cane, where the fungus is inserted at such a depth as not easily to be reached."

But in Burmah they had the same idea. There the coolies still light their cigarettes with a fire-piston. The Philippinos also use the same machine and ignite a wad of cotton stuck on the end of the piston by suddenly forcing the piston into air-tight cylinders, and when the piston is quickly withdrawn the cotton is found to be aflame, so it may be that the Colonial gentleman had traveled to the Indies and borrowed his idea from the Burmahs, or the Philippinos. At any rate we do not use it to-day in the woods, but it finds place here because it belongs to the friction fires and may be good as a suggestion for those among my readers of experimental and inventive minds.

CHAPTER II

FIRE MAKING BY PERCUSSION

THE WHITE MAN'S METHOD; HOW TO USE FLINT AND STEEL

WHERE TO OBTAIN THE FLINT AND STEEL

CHUCKNUCKS, PUNK BOXES, SPUNKS AND MATCHES

REAL LUCIFER MATCHES

SLOW MATCH

HOW TO CATCH THE SPARK

SUBSTITUTES FOR FLINT AND STEEL

CHAPTER II

FIRE MAKING BY PERCUSSION

THE preceding methods of producing fire by friction are not the white man's methods, and are not the methods used by our pioneer ancestors. The only case the writer can remember in which the pioneer white people used rubbing-sticks to produce fire, is one where the refugees from an Indian uprising and massacre in Oregon made fire from rubbing-sticks made of the bits of the splintered wood of a lightning stricken tree. On that occasion they evidently left home in a great hurry, without their flints and steels.

But this one instance in itself is sufficient to show to all outdoor people the great importance of the knowledge and ability to make friction fires. Like our good friend, the artist, explorer and author, Captain Belmore Browne, one may at any time get in a fix where one's matches are soaked, destroyed or lost and be compelled either to eat one's food raw or resort to rubbing-sticks to start a fire.

It is well, however, to remember that the flint and steel is

THE WHITE MAN'S METHOD

And notwithstanding the fire canes of our Colonial dudes, or the Pyropneumatic apparatus of the forgotten Mr. Bank, fire by percussion, that is, fire by friction of flint and steel, was universal here in America up to a quite recent date, and it is still in common use among many of my Camp-fire Club friends, and among many smokers.

How to Use Flint and Steel

In the age of flint and steel, the guns were all fired by this method. Fig. 33 shows the gun-lock of an old musket; the hammer holds a piece of flint, a small piece of buckskin is folded around the inside edge of the flint and serves to give a grip to the top part of the hammer which is screwed down. To fire the gun the hammer is pulled back at full cock, the steel sets opposite the hammer and is joined to the top of the powder-pan by a hinge. When the trigger is pulled the hammer comes down, striking the flint against the steel, throwing it back and exposing the powder at the same time to the sparks which ignite the powder in the gun by means of the touch hole in the side of the barrel of same. This is the sort of a hammer and lock used by all of our ancestors up to the time of the Civil War, and it is the sort of a hammer used by the Confederates as late as the battle of Fort Donaldson. In the olden times some people had flint lock pistols without barrels, which were used only to ignite punk for the purpose of fire-building. But when one starts a fire by means of flint and steel one's hands must act the part of the hammer, the back of one's knife may be the steel, then a piece of flint or a gritty rock and a piece of punk will produce the spark necessary to generate the flames.

In the good old pioneer days, when we all wore buckskin clothes and did not bother about the price of wool, when we wore coonskin caps and cared little for the price of felt hats, everybody, from Miles Standish and George Washington to Abraham Lincoln, used flint and steel. Fig. 27 shows ten different forms of steel used by our grandsires and granddames.

Flint in its natural condition may be found in many states, but, as a rule, any stone which was used by the Indians for

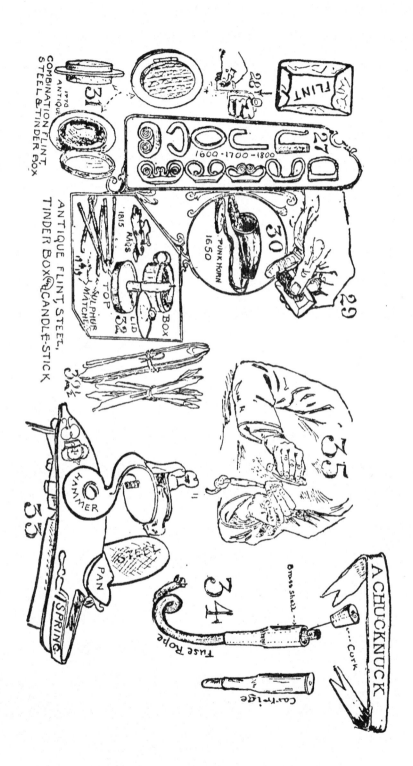

arrowheads will answer as a substitute for flint,* that is, any gritty or glassy stone, like quartz, agate, jasper or iron pyrites. Soft stones, limestones, slate or soapstones are not good for this purpose.

THE STEEL

Most of the old steels were so made that one might grasp them while thrusting one's fingers through the inside of the oval steel, Fig. 28 (left handed). Some of the Scoutmasters of the Boy Scouts of America make their own steels of broken pieces of flat ten-cent files, but this is unnecessary because every outdoor man, and woman, too, is supposed to carry a good sized jack-knife and the back of the blade of the jack-knife, or the back of the blade of one's hunting knife is good enough steel for anyone who has acquired the art of using it as a steel.

But if you must have steels manufactured at the machine shop or make them yourself, let them be an inch wide, a quarter of an inch thick, and long enough to form an ellipse like one of those shown in Fig. 27. Have the sharp edges rounded off. If you desire you may have your steel twisted in any of the shapes shown in Fig. 27 to imitate the ones used by your great granddaddies.

THE CHUCKNUCK

But the neatest thing in the way of flint and steel which has come to the writer's attention is shown by Fig. 31. This

---

* To-day flint may be obtained at Bannermans, 501 Broadway, New York City, where they also have ancient steels which were used by the U. S. soldiers. The flints may also be purchased from Wards Natural Science Establishment at Rochester, New York, and the author found a plentiful supply of flints at one of the Army and Navy stores in New York.

is a small German silver box which still contains some of the
original fungus used for punk and an ancient, well-battered
piece of flint. Around the box is fitted the steel in the form
of a band, and the whole thing is so small that it may be
carried in one's vest pocket. This was once the property of
Phillip Hagner, Lieutenant, of the City of Philadelphia at the
time of the Revolution, that is, custodian of city property.
He took the Christ Church bells from Philadelphia to Bethle-
hem by ox-cart before the city was occupied by the British.
Phillip Hagner came from Saxony about 1700 and settled in
Germantown, Philadelphia. This silver box was presented
to the National Scout Commissioner by Mr. Isaac Sutton,
Scout Commissioner for Delaware and Montgomery Coun-
ties, Boy Scouts of America.

PUNK BOXES

The cowhorn punk box is made by sawing off the small
end and then the point of a cow's horn (Fig. 30). A small
hole is next bored through the solid small end of the horn to
connect with the natural open space further down, a strip
of rawhide or whang string larger than the hole is forced
through the small end and secured by a knot on the inside,
which prevents it from being pulled out. The large end of the
horn is closed by a piece of thick sole leather attached to the
thong, by tying a hard knot in the end and pulling the thong
through a hole in the center of the stopper until the knot is
snug against the leather disk; this should be done before the
wet leather is allowed to dry. If the thong and leather stopper are made to fit the horn tightly, the dry baked rags, the
charred cotton, or whatever substance you use for punk,
when placed in the horn will be perfectly protected from
moisture or dampness.

SULPHUR HEADED SPUNKS AND MATCHES

These old sulphur "spunks" were nothing more than kindling wood or tinder, because they would not ignite by rubbing but were lighted by putting the sulphur end in the flame. According to our modern ideas of convenience they appear very primitive. They were called "spunks" in England and "matches" in America, and varied in length from three to seven inches, were generally packed in bundles from a dozen to two dozen and tied together with bits of straw. Some spunks made as late as 1830 are considered rare enough to be carefully preserved in the York Museum in England (Fig. 32½). The ones illustrated in Fig. 32 are a Long Island product, and were given to the author by the late John Halleran, the most noted antique collector on Long Island. These are carefully preserved among the antiquities in the writer's studio. But they are less than half the length of the ones formerly used on the Western Reserve. With the ancient matches in the studio are also two old pioneer tinder boxes with flints and steels. The tinder boxes are made of tin and contain a lot of baked rags. The inside lid acts as an extinguisher with which to cover up the punk or tinder in the box after you have lighted the candle in the tin lid of the box (Fig. 32).

The matches we use today are evolved from these old sulphur spunks. When the writer was a little fellow up in the Western Reserve on the shores of Lake Erie, he was intensely interested in an old lady making sulphur matches. Over the open fire she melted the sulphur in an iron kettle in which she dipped the ends of some pine slivers. The sulphur on the end of the sticks was then allowed to cool and harden. These matches were about the length of a lead pencil and could only be lighted by thrusting the sulphur into the flame. So, although having been born in the age of Lucifer matches, the writer was yet fortunate enough to see manufactured and to remember the contemporary ancestors of our present-day "safety" match.

The Real Lucifer Match

That is, the match which lights from friction, is the invention of Isaac Holden, M. P. According to the *Pall Mall Gazette*, Mr. Holden said, "In the morning I used to get up at 4 o'clock in order to pursue my studies, and I used at that time the flint and steel, in the use of which I found very great inconvenience. Of course, I knew, as other chemists did, the explosive material that was necessary in order to produce instantaneous light, but it was very difficult to obtain a light on wood by that explosive material, and the idea occurred to me to put sulphur under the explosive mixture. I did that and showed it in my next lecture on chemistry, a course of which I was delivering at a large academy."

Because every real woodsman is a student, as well as a sentimentalist, a brief history is given of these fire implements to entertain him as we jog along the "trace." All these things are blazes which mark the trail to the button in our wall which now produces the electric light. Some of them, like the clay cylinders found in the ruins of Babylon, are only useful in a historical sense, but many of them are essentially practical for woodcraft.

How to Make a Chucknuck

The slow match or punk rope to fit in the brass cylinder may be made of candle wick or coach wick purchased at the hardware store; such wick is about three-eighths of an inch in diameter. Scout Commissioner John H. Chase of Youngstown, Ohio, suggests that the rope may be made from the wastes of a machine shop or a garage; but one of the best woodsmen I know is Mr. Frederick K. Vreeland, and he uses the apparatus shown by Fig. 34, which is made of the yellow fuse rope, or punk rope, which may be purchased at cigar stores. He fastens a cork in one end of the rope by a wire, he pulls the other end of the rope through the end of the brass cartridge shell which has been filed off for that purpose. The end of the fuse rope must be charred, so as to catch the spark. To get the spark he takes the back of the blade of his knife (Fig. 35), and strikes the bit of flint as you would with flint and steel, holding the charred end of the punk against the flint, as shown by the diagram (Fig. 29). Loose cotton and various vegetable fibers twisted into a rope soaked in water and gunpowder will make good punk when dry.

To Get the Spark

Place the charred end of the rope on the flint, the charred portion about one thirty-second of an inch back of the edge of the flint where the latter is to be struck by the steel; hold the punk in place with the thumb of the left hand, as in the diagram (Fig. 29). Hold the knife about six inches above at an angle of about forty-five degrees from the flint, turn your knife so that the edge of the back of the blade will strike, then come down at an angle about thirty-five degrees with a sharp scraping blow. This should send the spark into the punk at the first or second blow. Now blow the punk until it is all aglow and you are ready to set your tinder afire. Push the punk into the middle of a handful of tinder and blow it until it is aflame, and the deed is done!

All these pocket contrivances for striking fire were formerly known as "striker-lights" or "chucknucks."

A Substitute for Flint and Steel

The Malays having neither flint nor steel ingeniously substitute for the flint a piece of broken chinaware, and for the steel a bamboo joint, and they produce a spark by striking the broken china against the joint of the bamboo, just as we do with the flint and steel.

CHAPTER III

HOW TO BUILD A FIRE

CHAPTER III

HOW TO BUILD A FIRE

"By thy camp-fire they shall know thee."

A PARTY of twenty or thirty men once called at the author's studio and begged that he would go with them on a hike, stating that they intended to cook their dinner out-of-doors. We went on the hike. The author asked the gentlemen to collect the wood for the fire; they did so enthusiastically and heaped up about a quarter of a cord of wood. There was no stick in the pile less than the thickness of one's arm, and many as thick as one's leg. A fine misty rain was falling and everything was damp. While all the other hikers gathered around, one of them carefully lighted a match and applied it to the heap of damp cord wood sticks. Match after match he tried, then turned helplessly to the writer with the remark, "It won't light, sir," and none there saw the humor of the situation!

Had anyone told the writer that from twenty-five to thirty men could be found, none of whom could build a fire, he would have considered the statement as highly improbable, but if he had been told that any intelligent man would try to light cord wood sticks, wet or dry, by applying a match to them, he would have branded the story as utterly beyond belief. It is, however, really astonishing how few people there are who know how to build a fire even when supplied with plenty of fuel and abundant matches.

MATCHES

It may be well to call the reader's attention to the fact that it takes very little moisture to spoil the scratch patch

35

on a box of safety matches and prevent the match itself from igniting. The so-called parlor match, which snaps when one lights it and often shoots the burning head into one's face or on one's clothes, is too dangerous a match to take into the woods. The bird's-eye match is exceedingly unreliable on the trail, but the old-fashioned, ill-smelling Lucifer match, sometimes called sulphur match, the kind

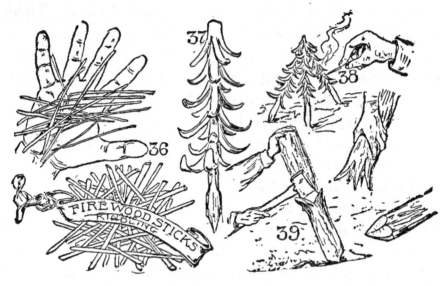

one may secure at the Hudson Bay Trading Post, the kind that comes in blocks and is often packed in tin cans, is the best match for woodcrafters, hunters, explorers, and hikers. Most of the outfitting stores in the big cities either have these matches or can procure them for their customers. When one of these matches is damp it may be dried by running it through one's hair.

Nowadays manual labor seems to be looked upon by everyone more in the light of a disgrace or punishment than as a privilege; nevertheless, it *is a privilege* to be able to labor, it *is a privilege* to have the vim, the pep, the desire and the ability to do things. Labor is a necessary attribute of the doer and those who live in the open; no one need attempt so simple a thing as the building of a fire and expect to succeed without labor.

One must use the axe industriously (Figs. 39, 42 and 43) in order to procure fuel for the fire; one must plan the fire carefully with regard to the wind and the inflammable material adjacent: one must collect and select the fuel intelligently.

The shirk, the quitter, or the side-stepper has no place in the open; his habitat is on the Great White Way among the Babylonians of the big cities. He does not even know the joys of a fire; he never sees a fire except when some building is burning. His body is heated by steam radiators, his food is cooked in some mysterious place beyond his ken, and brought to him by subservient waiters. He will be dead and flowers growing on his grave when the real fire-makers are just attaining the full vigor of their manhood.

Captain Belmore Browne says that the trails of the wilderness are its arteries; we may add that all trails proceed from camp or lead to camp, and that the camp-fire is the living, life-giving, palpitating heart of the camp; without it all is dead and lifeless. That is the reason that we of the outdoor brotherhood all love the fire; that is the reason that the odor of burning wood is incense to our nostrils; that is the reason that the writer cannot help talking about it when he should be telling

HOW TO BUILD A FIRE

Do not forget that lighting a fire in hot, dry weather is child's play, but that it takes a real camper to perform the same act in the damp, soggy woods on a cold, raw, rainy day, or when the first damp snow is covering all the branches of the trees and blanketing the moist ground with a slushy mantle of white discomfort! Then it is that fire making brings out all the skill and patience of the woodcrafter; nevertheless when he takes proper care neither rain, snow nor hail can spell failure for him.

Gummy Fagots of the Pine

In the mountains of Pennsylvania the old backwoodsmen, of which there are very few left, invariably build their fires with dry pine, or pitch pine sticks.

With their axe they split a pine log (Fig. 42), then cut it into sticks about a foot long and about the thickness of their own knotted thumbs, or maybe a trifle thicker (Fig. 40); after that they proceed to whittle these sticks, cutting deep shavings (Fig. 37), but using care to leave one end of the shavings adhering to the wood; they go round and round the stick with their knife blade making curled shavings until the piece of kindling looks like one of those toy wooden trees one used to find in his Noah's Ark on Christmas morning (Fig. 37).

When a backwoodsman finishes three or more sticks he sets them up wigwam form (Fig. 38). The three sticks having been cut from the centre of a pine log, are dry and maybe resinous, so all that is necessary to start the flame is to touch a match to the bottom of the curled shavings (Fig. 38).

Before they do this, however, they are careful to have a supply of small slivers of pitch pine, white pine or split pine knots handy (Fig. 36). These they set up around the shaved sticks, maybe adding some hemlock bark, and by the time it is all ablaze they are already putting on larger sticks of ash, black birch, yellow birch, sugar maple or oak.

For be it known that however handy pitch pine is for starting a fire, it is not the material used as fuel in the fire itself, because the heavy smoke from the pitch blackens up the cooking utensils, gives a disagreeable taste to the food,

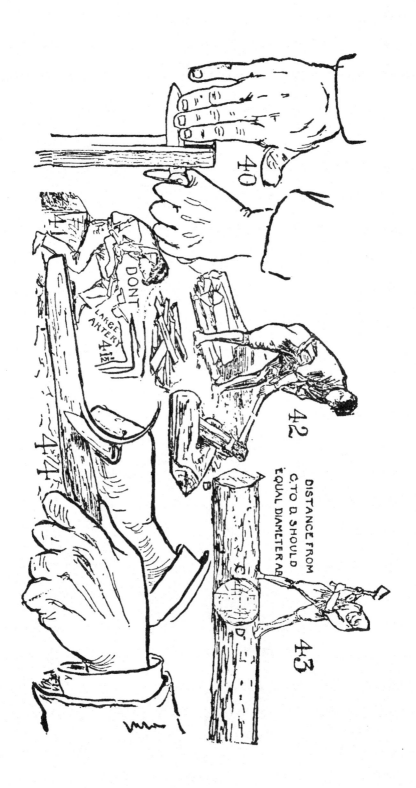

40

41

DON'T

LARGE
ARTERY
4 IN.

42

44

DISTANCE FROM
C. TO D. SHOULD
EQUAL DIAMETER A

43

spoils the coffee and is not a pleasant accompaniment even for a bonfire.

In the North woods, in the land of the birch trees, green birch bark is universally used as kindling with which to start a fire; green birch bark burns like tar paper. But whether one starts the fire with birch bark, shaved pine sticks or miscellaneous dry wood, one must remember that

Split Wood

Burns much better than wood in its natural form, and that logs from twelve to fourteen inches are best for splitting for fuel (Fig. 42); also one must not forget that in starting a fire the smaller the slivers of kindling wood are made, the easier it is to obtain a flame by the use of a single match (Fig. 36), after which the adding of fuel is a simple matter. A fire must have air to breathe in order to live, that is a draught, consequently kindling piled in the little wigwam shape is frequently used.

Fire-dogs

For an ordinary, unimportant fire the "turkey-lay" (Fig. 54) is handy, but for camp-fires and cooking fires we use andirons on which to rest the wood, but of course in the forests we do not call them andirons. They are not made of iron; they are either logs of green wood or stones and known to woodsmen by the name of "fire-dogs."

While we are on the subject of fire making it may be worth while to call the reader's attention to the fact that every outdoor person should know how to use a pocket knife, a jack-knife or a hunter's knife with the greatest efficiency and the least danger.

To those of us who grew up in the whittling age, it may seem odd or even funny that anyone should deem it necessary to tell how to open a pocket knife. But today I fail to recall to my mind a single boy of my acquaintance who knows how to properly handle a knife or who can whittle a stick with any degree of skill, and yet there are few men in this world with a larger acquaintance among the boys than myself. Not only is this true, but I spend two months of each year in the field with a camp full of boys, showing them how to do the very things with their knives and their axes described in this book.

How to Open a Knife

It is safe to say that when the old-timers were boys

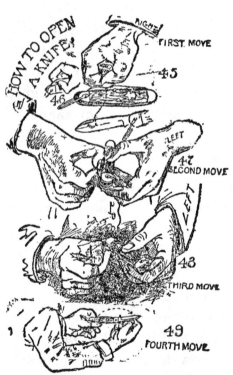

themselves, there was not a lad among them who could not whittle with considerable skill and many a twelve year old boy was an adept at the art. I remember with the keenest pleasure the rings, charms and knick-knacks which I carved with a pocket knife before I had reached the scout age of twelve. Today, however, the boys handle their knives so awkwardly as to make the chills run down the back of an onlooker.

In order to properly open a knife, hold it in your left hand, and with the thumbnail of your right hand grasp the blade at the nail notch (Fig. 45) in such a manner that the line of the nail makes a very slight angle; that is, it is as near perpendicular as may be (Fig. 46), otherwise you will bend back your thumbnail until it hurts or breaks. Pull the blade away from your body, at the same time drawing the handle of the knife towards the body (Figs. 47 and 48). Continue this movement until the blade is fully open and points directly from your body (Fig. 49).

Practise this and make it a habit; you will then never be in danger of stabbing yourself during the process of opening your knife—you will open a knife properly and quickly by what is generally termed intuition, but what is really the result of training and habit.

How to Whittle

The age of whittling began with the invention of the pocket knife and reached its climax about 1840 or '50, dying out some time after the Civil War, probably about 1870. All the old whittlers of the whittling age whittled *away* from the body. If you practise whittling that way it will become a habit.

Indians use a crooked knife and whittle towards the body, but the queer shape of their knife does away with the danger of an accidental stab or slash. Cobblers use a wicked sharp knife and cut towards their person and often are severely slashed by it, and sometimes dangerously wounded, because a big artery runs along the inside of one's leg (Fig. 41½) near where most of the scars on the cobbler's legs appear. When you whittle do not whittle with a stick between your legs as in Fig. 41, and always whittle away from you as in Fig. 44.

How to Split with a Jack-knife

Fig. 40 shows the proper way to use the knife in splitting a stick, so that it will not strain the spring at the back of the handle of the knife, and at the same time it will help you guide the knife blade and tend to make a straight split. Do not try to pry the stick apart with a knife or you will sooner or later break the blade, a serious thing for a wilderness man to do, for it leaves him without one of the most useful tools.

Remember that fine slivers of wood make a safer and more certain start for a fire than paper. All tenderfeet first try dry leaves and dry grass to start their fires. This they do because they are accustomed to the use of paper and naturally seek leaves or hay as a substitute for paper. But experience soon teaches them that leaves and grass make a nasty smudge or a quick, unreliable flame which ofttimes fails to ignite the wood, while, when proper care is used, small slivers of dry wood never fail to give satisfactory results.

There are many sorts of fires used by campers and all are dependent upon the local supply of fuel; in the deforested districts of Korea the people use twisted grass for fuel, on our Western plains the hunters formerly used buffalo chips and now they use cow chips, that is, the dry manure of cattle, with which to build their fires for cooking their meals and boiling their coffee. In the Zurn belt, in Tartary and Central India cattle manure is collected, piled up like cord wood and dried for fuel. A few years ago they used corn on the cob for firewood in Kansas. It goes without saying that buffalo chips are not good for bonfires or any fire where a big flame or illumination is an object.

BONFIRES AND COUNCIL FIRES

Are usually much larger than camp-fires, and may be made by heaping the wood up in conical form (Fig. 50) with the kindling all ready for the torch in the center of the pile, or the wood may be piled up log cabin style (Fig. 51) with the kindling underneath the first floor.

In both of these forms there are air spaces purposely left between the sticks of wood, which insure a quick and ready draught the moment the flames start to flicker in the kindling.

The best form of council fire is shown by Fig. 52, and known as the

CAMP MEETING TORCH

Because it was from a somewhat similar device at a camp meeting in Florida, that the author got the suggestion for his "torch fire." The platform is made of anything handy and is covered with a thick flooring of sod, sand or clay for the fire-place.

The tower is built exactly similar to the Boy Scout signal towers but on a smaller scale (Fig. 52).

DANGER OF EXPLODING STONES

However tempting a smooth rock may look as a convenient spot on which a fire may be built, do not fail to spread a few shovels of sand, earth or clay on the stone as a fire bed, for the damp rock on becoming heated may generate steam and either expand with some violence or burst like a bombshell and scatter far and wide the fragments, even endangering the lives of those gathered around the fire.

CHARACTER IN FIRE

The natives of Australia take dry logs, 6 ft. or more in length, and laying them down 3 ft. or 4 ft. apart, set them on fire in several places. Letting shorter logs meet them from the outside, and placing good-sized pebbles around them, they then stretch themselves on the ground and sleep between the two lines of fire, and when the wood is consumed the stones continue for some time to radiate the heat they have previously absorbed. Many tribes of American Indians have their own special fashion of fire building, so that a deserted camp fire will not infrequently reveal the identity of the tribe by which it was made.

SLOW FIRES

The camper's old method of making a slow fire was also used by housekeepers for their open fire-places, and consisted of placing three logs with their glowing ends together.

As the ends of the logs burned off the logs were pushed forward, this being continued until the logs were entirely consumed. Three good logs thus arranged will burn all day or all night, but someone must occasionally push them so that their ends come together, when they send their heat from one to the other, backwards and forwards, and thus keep the embers hot (Fig. 53). But who wants to sit up all night watching a fire? I prefer to use the modern method and sleep all night.

Sharpen the ends of two strong heavy stakes each about 5 ft. in length, cut a notch in the rear of each near the top, for the support or back to key into, drive the stakes into the ground about 6 ft. apart. Place three logs one on the other, making a log wall for the back of your fire-place. Next take two shorter logs and use them for fire-dogs, and on these lay another log and the arrangement will be complete. A fire of this kind will burn during the longest night and if skillfully made will cause little trouble. The fire is fed by placing fuel between the front log and the fire-back.

SIGNAL FIRES

When the greatest elevations of land are selected the smoke signals may be seen at a distance of from twenty to fifty miles. Signal fires are usually made with dry leaves, grass and weeds or "wiry willows," balsam boughs, pine and cedar boughs, because such material produces great volumes of smoke and may be seen at a long distance. The Apaches have a simple code which might well be adopted by all outdoor people. According to J. W. Powell, Director of U. S. Bureau of Ethnology, the Indians use but three kinds of signals, each of which consists of columns of smoke.

Alarm

Three or more smoke columns reads impending danger from flood, fire or foe. This signal may be communicated from one camp to another, so as to alarm a large section of the country in remarkably quick time. The greater the haste desired the greater the number of smokes used. These fires are often so hastily made that they may resemble puffs of smoke caused by throwing heaps of grass and leaves upon the embers again and again.

Attention

"This signal is generally made by producing one continuous column and signifies attention for several purposes, viz., when a band had become tired of one locality, or the grass may have been consumed by the ponies, or some other cause necessitated removal, or should an enemy be reported which would require further watching before a decision as to future action would be made. The intention or knowledge of anything unusual would be communicated to neighboring bands by causing one column of smoke to ascend."

Establishment of a Camp, Quiet, Safety

"When a removal of camp has been made, after the signal for Attention has been given, and the party have selected a place where they propose to remain until there may be a necessity or desire for their removal, two columns of smoke are made, to inform their friends that they propose to remain at that place. Two columns are also made at other times during a long continued residence, to inform the neighboring bands that a camp still exists, and that all is favorable and quiet."

Therefore, THREE or more smokes in daylight, or THREE or more flames at night, is a signal of alarm, ONE smoke a signal for attention, Two smokes tells us that all is well, peaceful and happy.

SMOKE SIGNALS

The usual way of signalling with smoke is to make a smudge fire of browse or grass and use a blanket as an extinguisher. By covering the fire with the blanket and suddenly removing it, a large globular puff of smoke is made to suddenly appear, and is certain to attract the attention of anyone who happens to be looking toward the site of the fire.

HOW TO BUILD A FIRE ON THE SNOW

If it is practical it is naturally better to shovel away the snow, but personally I have never done this except in case of newly fallen snow. Old snow which is more or less frozen to the ground may be tramped down until it is hard and then covered with a corduroy of sticks for a hearth (Figs. 55 and 56) or with bark (Fig. 57) and on top of this flooring it is a simple matter to build a fire. Use the turkey-"lay" in which one of the sticks acts the part of the fire-dog (Fig. 56).

Don't fail to collect a generous supply of small wood (Fig. 58) and then start the fire as already directed (Fig. 58).

The reader will note that in all these illustrations (Figs. 55, 56 and 57), there is either a log or stone or a bank for a back to the fire-place. When everything is covered with snow it is perfectly safe to use a log for a back (Fig. 56) but on other occasions the log may smoulder for a week and then start a forest fire.

No one but an arrant, thoughtless, selfish Cheechako will use a live growing tree against which to build a fire.

A real woodcraft knows that a fire can ruin in a few minutes a mighty forest tree that God himself cannot replace inside of from forty to one hundred years.

While we are talking of building fires in the snow, it may be well to remark that an uninhabitable and inaccessible swamp in the summer is often the best of camping places in the winter time. The water freezes and falls lower and lower, leaving convenient shelves of ice (Fig. 57) for one's larder. The dense woods and brush offer a splendid barrier to the winter winds. Fig. 59 shows an arrangement for a winter camp-fire.

How to Make a Fire in the Rain

Spread a piece of bark on the ground to serve as a hearth on which to start your fire. Seek dry wood by splitting the log and taking the pieces from the center of the wood, keep the wood under cover of your tent, poncho, coat or blanket. Also hold a blanket or some similar thing over the fire while you are lighting it. After the blaze begins to leap and the logs to burn freely, it will practically take a cloud-burst to extinguish it.

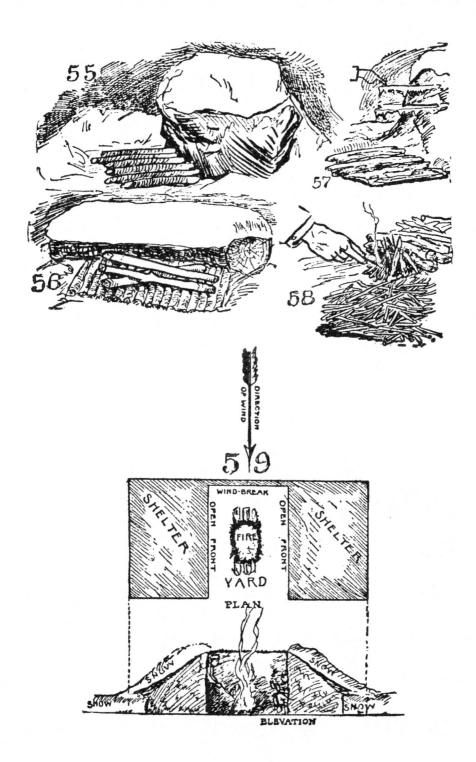

CHAPTER IV

HOW TO LAY A GOOD COOKING FIRE

CHAPTER IV

HOW TO LAY A GOOD COOKING FIRE

No matter where the old camper may be, no matter how long a time may have elapsed since last he slept in the open, no matter how high or low a social or official position he may now occupy, it takes but one whiff of the smoke of an open fire, or one whiff of the aroma of frying bacon, to send him back again to the lone trail. In imagination he will once more be hovering over his little camp-fire in the desert, under the shade of the gloomy pines, mid the snows of Alaska, in the slide rock of the Rockies or mid the pitch pines of the Alleghenies, as the case may be.

That faint hint in the air of burning firewood or the delicious odor of the bacon, for the moment, will not only wipe from his vision his desk, his papers and his office furniture, but also all the artificialities of life. Even the clicking of the typewriter will turn into the sound of clicking hoofs, the streets will become canyons, and the noise of traffic the roar of the mountain torrent!

There is no use talking about it, there is no use arguing about it, there *is* witchcraft in the smell of the open fire, and all the mysteries and magic of the Arabian Nights dwell in the odor of frying bacon.

Some years ago Mr. Arthur Rice, the Secretary of the Camp-fire Club of America, and Patrick Cleary, a half-breed Indian, with the author, became temporarily separated from their party in the Northern wilds. They found themselves on a lonely wilderness lake surrounded by picture mountains, and dotted with tall rocky islands covered with Christmas trees, giving the whole landscape the appearance of the scenery one sometimes sees painted on drop-curtains for the theatre. Everything in sight was grand, everything was beautiful, everything was built on a generous scale, everything was big, not forgetting the voyagers' appetites!

Unfortunately the provisions were in the missing canoe; diligent search, however, in the bottom of Patrick Cleary's ditty bag disclosed three small, hard, rounded lumps, which weeks before might have been bread; also a handful of tea mixed with smoking tobacco, and that was all! There was no salt, no butter, no pepper, no sugar, no meat, no knives, no forks, no spoons, no cups, no plates, no saucers and no cooking utensils; the party had nothing but a few stone-like lumps of bread and the weird mixture of tea and tobacco with which to appease their big appetites. But in the lake the trout were jumping, and it was not long before the hungry men had secured a fine string of spotted beauties to add to their menu.

Under the roots of a big spruce tree, at the bottom of a cliff on the edge of the lake, a fountain of cold crystal water spouted from the mossy ground. Near this they built a fire while Mr. Rice fashioned a little box of birch bark, filled it with water and placed it over the hot embers by resting the ends of the box on fire-dogs of green wood. Into the water in the birch bark vessel was dumped the tea (and— also tobacco)!

To the amazement and delight of the Indian half-breed, the tea was soon boiling. Meanwhile the half-breed toasted some trout until the fish were black, this being done so that the charcoal or burnt skins might give a flavor to the fish, and in a measure compensate for the lack of salt. The hunks of bread were burned until they were black, not for flavor this time. but in order that the bread might be brittle enough to allow a man to bite into it with no danger of breaking his teeth in the attempt.

To-day it seems to the author that that banquet on that lonely lake, miles from the nearest living human being, was more delicious and more satisfying than any of the feasts of Belshazzar he has since attended in the wonder city of New York.

Therefore, when taking up the subject of cooking fire and camp kitchen, he naturally begins with

The Most Primitive of Cooking Outfits

Consisting of two upright forked sticks and a wangan-stick to lay across from fork to fork over the fire. Or maybe a speygelia-stick thrust slantingly into the ground in front of the fire, or perhaps a saster-pole on which to suspend or from which to dangle, in front of the fire, a hunk of moose meat, venison, mountain sheep, mountain goat, whale blubber, beaver, skunk, rabbit, muskrat, woodchuck, squirrel or whatsoever fortune may send.

Camp Pot-hooks

Are of various forms and designs, but they are not the S shaped things formerly so familiar in the big open fire-places of the old homesteads, neither are they the hated S shaped marks with which the boys of yesterday were wont to struggle and disfigure the pages of their writing books.

If any one of the camp pot-hooks had been drawn in the old-time writing book or copybook, it would have brought down the wrath (with something else) of the old-fashioned school-master, upon the devoted head of the offending pupil. For these pot-hooks are not regular in form and the shape and designs largely depend upon the available material from which they are fashioned, and not a little upon the individual fancy of the camper. For instance the one known as

The Gallow-crook

Is not, as the name might imply, a human crook too intimately associated with the gallows, but on the contrary it is a rustic and useful bit of forked stick (Figs. 60, 61, 62 and 63) made of a sapling. Fig. 60 shows how to select the sapling and where to cut it below a good sturdy fork. Fig. 61 shows the bit of sapling trimmed down to the proper length and with two forks, one at each end. On the upper fork you will note that one prong is a slender elastic switch. Fig. 62 shows how this switch may be bent down and bound with a string or tape made of green bark, and so fastened to the main stem as to form a loop which will easily slip over the waugan-stick as in Fig. 63. Fig. 62A shows a handy hitch with which to make fast the bark binding.

When the wangan-stick has been thrust through the loop of the gallow-crook, the former is replaced in the crotches of the two forked sticks, as in Fig. 63, and the pot or kettle, pail or bucket, is hooked on to the lower fork. You will note that the lower fork is upon the opposite side of the main stick from that from which the switch prong of the upper fork springs. This arrangement is not necessary to make the pot balance properly over the fire; the same rule holds good for all the other pot-hooks.*

The Pot-claw

Will be best understood by inspecting the diagrams (Figs. 64, 65 and 66), which show its evolution or gradual growth. By these diagrams you will see the stick is so cut that the

---

* The pots will balance better if the notches are on the same side.

64 67 65 63 66 68 69

A GALLOW-CROOK POT-CLAW THE HAKE THE GIB WAUGAN-STICK B

69A

THE GIB

70

60 61 72

A 62

SASTER 74 SPEYGELIA

SPEYGELIA 73 71

fork may be hooked over the wangan-stick and the cooking utensils, pots or kettles may be hung over the fire by slipping their handles into the notch cut in the stick on the side opposite to the fork and near the lower end of the pot-claw. This is a real honest-to-goodness Buckskin or Sourdough pot-hook; it is one that requires little time to manufacture and one that is easily made wherever sticks grow, or wherever "whim" sticks or driftwood may be found heaped upon the shore.

THE HAKE

Is easier to make than the pot-claw. It is a forked stick like the pot-claw, but in place of the notch near the lower end a nail is driven diagonally into the stick and the kettle hung on the nail (Figs. 67 and 68). The hake possesses the disadvantage of making it necessary for the camper to carry a supply of nails in his kit. No Sourdough on a long and perilous trip loads himself down with nails. A hake, however, is a very good model for Boy Scouts, Girl Pioneers, and hikers of all descriptions who may go camping in the more thickly settled parts of the country.

THE GIB

Is possibly a corruption of gibbet, but it is a much more humane implement. It requires a little more time and a little more skill to make a gib (Fig. 69) than it does to fashion the preceding pot-hook. It is a useful hook for stationary camps where one has time to develop more or less intricate cooking equipment. Fig. 69A shows how the two forked sticks are cut to fit together in a splice, and it also shows how this splice is nailed together with a couple of wire nails, and **Fig. 70** shows how the wire nails are clinched.

In a book of this kind the details of all these designs are given not because any one camper is expected to use them all, but because there are times when any one of them may be just the thing required. It is well, however, to say that the most practicable camp pot-hooks are the pot-claw and the hake.

In making a pot-claw care should be taken to cut the notch on the opposite side of the forked branch, and at the other end of the claw, deep enough to hold the handle of the cooking utensils securely.

While the author was on an extended trip in the blustering North land his party had a pot-claw as crooked as a yeggman, and as knotty as a problem in higher mathematics. While there can be no doubt that one of the party made this hoodoo affair it has never yet been decided to whom the credit belongs—because of the innate modesty of the men no one claims the honor. This misshapen pot-claw was responsible for spilling the stew on several occasions, not to speak of losing the boiled rice. Luckily one of the party was a stolid Indian, one a consistent member of the Presbyterian church, one a Scout and one a member of the Society of Friends, consequently the air *was not blue* and the only remarks made were, "Oh my!" "Bless my soul!" and "Gee willikens!"

The cook in despair put the wicked thing in the fire with muttered hints that the fire might suggest the region where such pot-hooks belong. While it burned and its evil spirit dissolved in smoke, the Indian made a new pot-claw, a respectable pot-claw with a straight character, and a more secure notch. This one by its benign presence brought peace and good will to the camp and showed the necessity of taking pains and using care in the manufacture of even so lowly a thing as a pot-claw.

The camp pot-hooks should be of various lengths; long

ones to bring the vessels near the fire where the heat is more intense; short ones to keep the vessels further from the fire so that their contents will not cook but only keep warm; and medium ones for simmering or slow cooking.

THE SPEYGELIA

Is not an Italian, but is a long name for a short implement. The speygelia is a forked stick or a notched stick (Figs. 71, 72 and 73), which is either propped up on a forked stick (Fig. 71) and the lower end held down by a stone in such a manner that the fork at the upper end offers a place to hang things over, or in front of the fire, sometimes a notched stick is used in the same manner as Fig. 73. Where the ground is soft to permit it, the stick is driven diagonally into the earth, which may hold it in place without other support. The speygelia is much used by cow-punchers and other people in places where wood is scarce.

THE SASTER

The saster is a long pole used in the same manner as the speygelia. Meat is suspended from it in front of the fire to roast (Figs. 74½ and 75), or kettles are suspended from it over the fire to boil water (Fig. 74).

TELEGRAPH WIRE COOKING IMPLEMENTS

Many campers are fond of making for themselves cooking utensils improvised from ordinary telegraph wire. In the old time open fireplaces of our grandsires' kitchen there were trammels consisting of chains hanging down the chimney on which things were hooked by short pot-hooks to hang over the fire; there were also rakens made of bands of iron with holes punched in them for the attachment of short iron pot-hooks (Fig. 76). With these ancient implements in their minds, some ingenious campers manufacture themselves rakens and short pot-hooks from telegraph wire (Fig. 77). By twisting the wire in a series of short loops, each loop can be made to serve as a place for attaching the pot-hooks as did the holes in the old-fashioned rakens. The advantages they claim for the telegraph wire raken are lightness and its possibility of being readily packed.

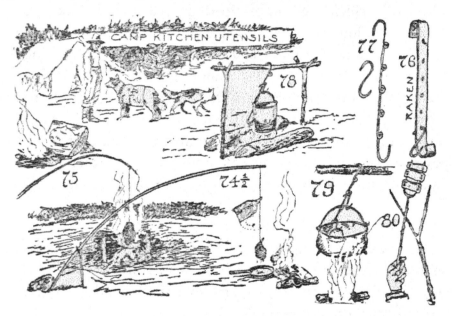

On one of these rakens one may hook the pail as high or as low as one chooses (Fig. 78); not only that but one may (Fig. 79) put a small pail inside the larger one, where later it is full of water, for the purpose of cooking cereal without danger of scorching it.

The disadvantage of all these implements is that they must be toted wherever one goes, and parts are sure to be lost sooner or later, whereupon the camper must resort to things "with the bark on 'em," like the gallow-crook, the pot-claw, the hake, the gib, the speygelia, or the saster, or

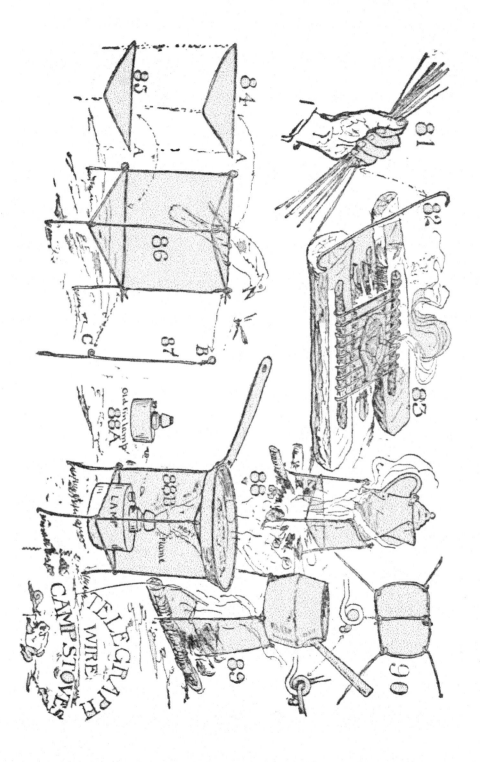

he may go back to the first principles and sharpen the forks of a green wand and impale thereon the bacon, game or fish that it may be thus toasted over the hot embers (Fig. 80). We do not put meat *over* the fire because it will burn on the outside before it cooks and the fumes of the smoke will spoil its flavor.

According to Mr. Seton, away up in the barren lands they use the saster with a fan made of a shingle-like piece of wood, fastened with a hitch to a piece of wire and a bit of string; the wind—when it is good-natured—will cause the cord to spin round and round. But the same result is secured with a cord which has been soaked in water to prevent it from burning, and which has also been twisted by spinning the meat with one's hands (Fig. 75). Such a cord will unwind and wind more or less slowly for considerable time, thus causing the meat to expose all sides of its surface to the heat of the roasting fire in front of which it hangs. You will note we say in front; again let us impress upon the reader's mind that he must not hang his meat over the flame. In Fig. 75 the meat is so drawn that one might mistake its position and think it was intended to hang over the fire, whereas the intention is to hang it in *front* of the fire as in Fig. 74. In the writer's boyhood days it was his great delight to hang an apple by a wet string in front of the open fire, and to watch it spin until the heat sent the juices bubbling through the skin and the apple gradually became thoroughly roasted.

The Gridiron

Campers have been known to be so fastidious as to demand a broiler to go with their kit; at the same time there was enough of the real camper in them to cause them to avoid carrying unwieldy broilers such as are used

in our kitchens. Consequently they compromise by packing a handful of telegraph wires of even length with
their duffel (Fig. 81), each wire having its ends carefully
bent in the form of a hook (Fig. 82), which may be adjusted over two green sticks resting upon two log fire-dogs
(Fig. 83), and upon the wires, so arranged, meat and fish
may be nicely broiled.

This is not a bad scheme, but the campers should have a
little canvas bag in which they may pack the wires, otherwise the camper will sooner or later throw them away rather
than be annoyed by losing one every now and then. Figs.
84, 85, 86, 87 and 88 show a little

Skeleton Camp Stove

Ingeniously devised by a Boy Pioneer. Two pieces of telegraph wire are bent into a triangular form (Figs. 84 and 85),
and the ends of the triangle at A are left open or unjoined,
so that they may readily be slipped through the loops in the
upright wires, B and C (Fig. 87), and thus form a take-a-part
skeleton stove (Fig. 86). The young fellow from whom this
device was obtained was at the time using an old tin kerosene-
lamp (Fig. 88A) which he forced into the lower triangle of the
stove (Fig. 86), and which the spring of the wire of the triangle held in position (Fig. 88B).

But if one is going to use the telegraph wire camp stove
there is no necessity of carrying a lamp. The stove is made
so that it may be taken apart and packed easily and the
weight is trifling, but a lamp of any kind, or even a lantern,
is a nuisance to carry.

The telegraph wire camp stove, however, may be made
by bending the wires as shown in Fig. 90, but the only object
in so doing is to develop one's ingenuity, or for economy sake,

otherwise one may purchase at the outfitter's folding wire camp broilers for a trifle, made on the same principle and with legs which may be thrust into the ground surrounding the fire, as in Figs. 88 and 89, and, after the broiler is folded in the middle, the legs may be folded back so that it will all make a flat package. But leaving the artificialities of tele-graph wire let us go back to the real thing again and talk about laying and lighting a genuine

Camp Cooking Fire

The more carefully the fire is planned and built the more easily will the cooking be accomplished. The first thing to be considered in laying one of these fires is the

Fire-dogs

Which in camp are the same as andirons in the open fire-places. of our homes, and used for the same purpose. But domestic andirons are heavy steel bars usually with ornamental brass uprights in front and they would be most unhandy for one to carry upon a camping trip, while it would be the height of absurdity to think of taking andirons on a real hunting or exploring expedition. Therefore, we use green logs, sods or stones for fire-dogs in the wilderness. Frequently we have a back-log against which the fire-dog rests; this back log is shown in Fig. 91. In this particular case it acts both as a back log and a fire-dog. In the plan just above it (Fig. 92), there are two logs side by side which serve the double pur-pose of fire-dogs and for sides of the kitchen stove (Fig. 93). Fig. 94 shows

The Lay of a Roasting Fire

Sometimes called the round fire. The back is laid up log-cabin style and the front is left open. In the open enclosure

the fire is built by sticks being laid up like those in **Fig. 91.**
The logs on all three sides radiate the heat and when the meat
is hung in front of this, suspended from the end of the saster
(Fig. 74½), it is easily and thoroughly roasted.

THE CAMP-FIRE

Is built with an eye to two purposes: one is to reflect heat
into the open tent in front, and the other is to so construct
it that it may last a long time. When one builds a camp-fire
one wants to be able to roll up in one's blanket and sleep with
the comforting conviction that the fire will last until morning.

The camp-fire is made with two fire-dogs pushed back
against a back log (Fig. 95A and B), which form the foundation for the camp-fire. Two upright green sticks C (Fig. 95)
are placed in a slanting position and supported by other
sticks, D (Fig. 95), the top ends of which rest in notches cut
in C stick at E (Fig. 95), and the bottom ends of which are
thrust into the ground. Against the upright sticks C, and
the logs F are heaped to form the back of the fire. The fire
is then built on the two fire-dogs AA, and against the F logs,
the latter will burn slowly and at the same time reflect the
heat into the open tent front. This same fire is sometimes
used for a baking fire, but the real fire for this purpose is
made by the

BELMORE LAY

Figs. 96 and 97. The first sketch shows the plan and the
second the perspective view of the fire. The stove is made
by two side logs or fire-dogs over which the fire is built and
after it has fallen in, a mass of red hot embers, between the
fire-dogs, two logs are laid across the dogs and one log is
placed atop, so that the flame then comes up in front of them
(Fig. 97) and sends the heat against the bread or bannock.

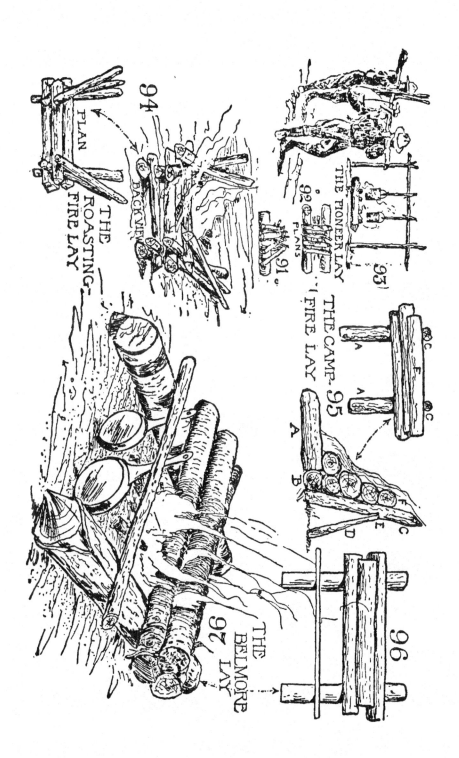

94

PLAN

BACK VIEW

THE
ROASTING
FIRE LAY

THE PIONEER LAY

92
PLANS

91

93

THE CAMP 95
FIRE LAY

A C
E
A
C
B

A
B
F
C
E
D

THE
BELMORE
LAY 97

96

At a convenient distance in front of the fuel logs, a waugan-stick is placed, reaching from one fire-dog to the other.

In wilderness work the frying pan is about the only domestic utensil carried and is used as a toaster, a baker, a broiler, a fryer, and a stew pan all combined. In it the Buckskin man and the Sourdough make their bread, and after the bread has been baked over the coals on the bottom, it is browned nicely on its top by tilting the pans in front of the fire and resting their handles against the waugan-stick (Fig. 97). I have seen the baking fire used from British Columbia to Florida, but it was the explorer, Captain Belmore Browne, who showed me the use of the waugan-stick in connection with the baking fire, hence I have called this the Belmore Lay.

A FRYING FIRE

Is built between two logs, two rows of stones, or sods (Figs. 98, 99 and 100); between these logs the fire is usually built, using the sides as fire-dogs, or the sticks may be placed in the turkey-lay (Fig. 100), so that the sticks themselves make a fire-dog and allow, for a time, a draught until the fire is burning briskly, after which it settles down to hot embers and is in the proper condition for frying. For be it known that too hot a griddle will set the grease or bacon afire, which may be funny under ordinary circumstances, but when one is shy of bacon it is a serious thing. The

ORDINARY BAKING FIRE LAY

Is shown by Fig. 101. In this instance, the frying pans being used as reflector ovens are propped up by running sticks through the holes in their handles.

The Aures

Is a rustic crane made exactly of the same form as are the cranes of the old-fashioned open fire-places, but ingeniously fashioned from a carefully selected green stick with two forks (Fig. 102). The long end of the main branch is severed at A (Fig. 102), care being taken not to cut through the green bark, B (Fig. 102). The bark of the latter, B, is then bent over the stub, A (Fig. 102), forming a loop, C (Fig. 103), which is lashed with green bark to the main stick and slipped over the upright, D (Fig. 104). The fork at E braces the crane and holds it in a horizontal position, resting on a stub left on D for that purpose. How practicable this thing may be depends altogether upon the time and skill one has at one's disposal. One would hardly use the Aures for a single night camp, but if one were to spend a week in the same camp, it would be well worth while and at the same time very interesting work to manufacture a neat Aures crane for the camp kitchen. The next step in camp kitchen fires will include what might be termed the pit fires, which will be described in the following chapter.

You have been told how to select the firewood, make the kindling and start a fire in the preceding chapter on how to build a fire; all you have to remember now is that in certain particulars *all* fires are alike; they all must have *air* to breathe and *food* to eat or they will not live.

In the case of the fire we do not call the air breath, but we give it a free circulation and call it a draught. Wood is the food that the fire eats and it must be digestible, a fire with indigestion is a fire fed with punky, damp wood carelessly thrown together in place of well-selected dry split wood which the fire can consume cleanly, digest evenly, and at the same time give out the greatest amount of heat.

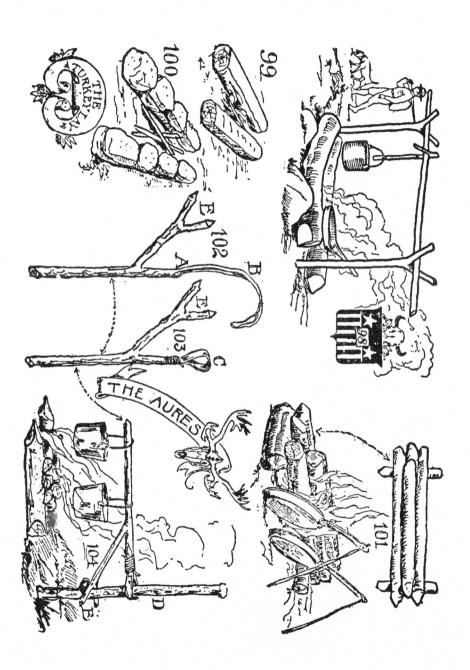

To produce a draught the fire must, of course, be raised from the ground, but do not build it in a careless manner like a pile of jack-straws. Such a fire may start all right, but when the supporting sticks have burned away it will fall in a heap and precipitate the cooking utensils into the flames, upsetting the coffee or teapot, and dumping the bacon "from the frying pan into the fire."

Be it man, woman, boy or girl, if he, she or it expects to be a camper, he, or she or it must learn to be orderly and tidy around camp. No matter how soiled one's clothes may be, no matter how grimy one's face may look, the ground around the camp-fire must be clean, and the cooking utensils and fire wood, pot-hooks and wangan-sticks, all orderly and as carefully arranged as if the military officer was expected the next minute to make an inspection.

All my readers must remember that BY THEIR CAMP-FIRE THEY WILL BE KNOWN and "sized up" as the real thing or as chumps, duffers, tenderfeet and cheechakos, by the first Sourdough or old-timer who cuts their trails.

CHAPTER V

CAMP KITCHENS.

CAMP PIT-FIRES, BEAN HOLES

COW-BOY FIRE-HOLE

CHINOOK COOKING FIRE-HOLE

BARBECUE-FITS

THE GOLD DIGGER'S OVEN

THE FERGUSON CAMP STOVE

THE ADOBE OVEN

THE ALTAR CAMPFIRE PLACE

CAMP KITCHEN FOR HIKERS, SCOUTS,
    EXPLORERS, SURVEYORS AND HUNTERS

HOW TO COOK MEAT, FISH AND BREAD
    WITHOUT POTS, PANS OR STOVES

DRESSING SMALL ANIMALS

HOW TO BARBECUE LARGE ANIMALS

CHAPTER V

CAMP KITCHENS

REAL camp kitchens are naught but well arranged fire-places with rustic cranes and pot-hooks as already described, but in deforested countries, or on the plains and prairies, pit-fires are much in vogue. The pit itself shelters the fire on the windswept plain, which is doubly necessary because of the unprotected nature of such camping places, and because of the kind of fuel used. Buffalo-chips were formerly used on the Western plains, but they are now superseded by cattle chips. The buffalo-chip fire was the cooking fire of the Buck-skin-clad long-haired plainsmen and the equally picturesque cowboy; but the buffalo herds have long since hit the trail over the Great Divide where all tracks point one way, the sound of the thunder of their feet has died away forever, as has also the whoop of the painted Indians. The romantic and picturesque plainsmen and the wild and rollicking cow-boys have followed the herds of buffalo and the long lines of prairie schooners are a thing of the past, but the pit-fires of the hunters are still in use.

THE MOST SIMPLE PIT-FIRE

Is a shallow trench dug in the ground, on each side of which two logs are placed; in the pit between the logs a fire is built (Fig. 105), but probably the most celebrated pit-fire is the fireless cooker of the camp, known and loved by all under the name of

THE BEAN HOLE

Fig. 106 shows a half section of a bean hole lined with stones. The bean hole may, however, be lined with clay or

6

simply the damp earth left in its natural state. This pit-fire place is used differently from the preceding one, for in the bean hole the fire is built and burns until the sides are heated good and hot, then the fire is removed and the bean pot put in place, after which the whole thing is covered up with ashes and earth and allowed to cook at its leisure.

The Cowboy Pit-fire

The cowboy pit-fire is simply a trench dug in the earth (Fig. 107), with a basin-shaped hole at the beginning. When obtainable, sticks are laid across the trench and sods laid upon the top of the sticks. Fig. 107 shows a section of view of the pit-fire and trench chimney, and Fig. 108 shows the top view of the same.

In removing the sod one should be careful not to break them, then even though there be no sticks one may be able to cover the draught chimney with the sods themselves by allowing them to bridge the trench. At the end of the trench the sods are built up, making a short smokestack.

The Chinook Fire-pit

The chinook fire-pit is one which is used in the north-western part of the United States, and seems to be a combination of the ordinary camp fire-dogs with cross logs and the cowboy fire-pit. Fig. 109 shows a perspective view of this lay. Fig. 110 shows the top view of plan of the lay. Fig. 111 shows a steeper perspective view than that of Fig. 109, and Fig. 112 shows a sectional view. By examining the sectional view and also the deeper perspective view, as well as the plan, you will note that the two logs are placed across the fire-dogs with space between. The back-log is placed upon the top of another back-log A and B (Fig. 112). The fire-dogs have

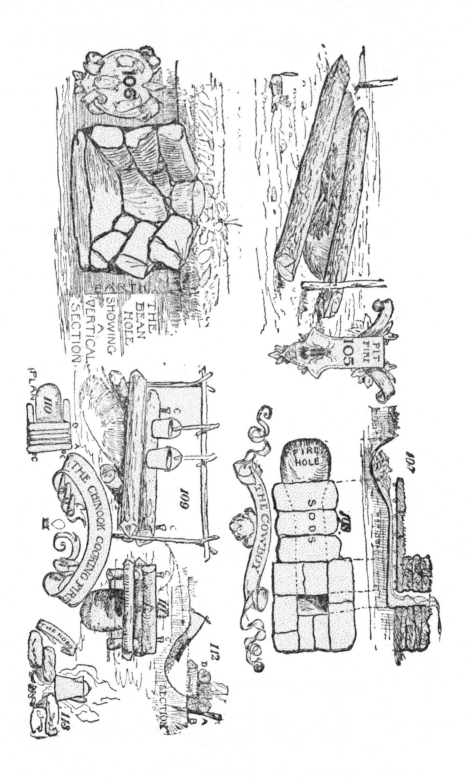

THE BEAN HOLE SHOWING A VERTICAL SECTION.

PIT FIRE
105

THE COWBOY

FIRE HOLE

SODS

107

108

THE CHINOOK COOKING FIRE

PLAN
110

109

THE HOBO

113

SECTION
112

their ends shoved against the bottom back-logs B, the two back-logs are kept in place by the stakes C, C. Between the two top logs D and A (Figs. 112 and 110), the smaller fuel or split wood is placed.

As the fire burns the hot coals drop into the pit, and when sufficient quantity of embers are there they may be raked forward and the frying pan placed on top of them (Fig. 112). The chinook fire is good for baking, frying, broiling, toasting, and is an excellent all-around kitchen camp stove.

THE HOBO

Is carelessly built, a fire-place usually surrounding a shallow pit, the sides built up with sods or stones. The hobo answers for a hasty fire over which to boil the kettle (Fig. 113).

At the old-fashioned barbecue where our ancestors roasted whole oxen, the ox was placed on a huge spit, which was turned with a crank handle, very similar to the old-fashioned well handle as used with a rope or chain and bucket.

THE BARBECUE-PIT

Is used at those feasts (Fig. 114), where they broil or roast a whole sheep, deer or pig. At a late meet of the Camp-fire Club of America they thus barbecued a pig.

The fire-pit is about four feet wide and four feet deep and is long enough (Fig. 114) to allow a fire to be built at each end of the pit, there being no fire under the meat itself for the very good reason that the melted fat would drop into the fire, cause it to blaze up, smoke and spoil the meat.

The late Homer Davenport (the old-time and famous cartoonist) some years ago gave a barbecue at his wild animal farm in New Jersey. When Davenport was not drawing cartoons he was raising wild animals. At the Davenport

barbecue there was a fire-pit dug in the side of the bank
(Fig. 115); such an arrangement is known as

THE BANK-PIT

In the diagram it will be seen that the carcass is fastened
to a spit of green wood, which runs thru a hole in a cross log

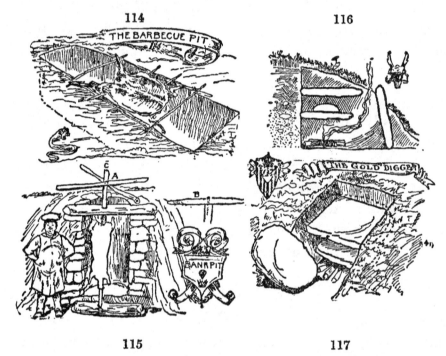

114   116

115   117

and fits in the socket D in the bottom log; the spit is turned
by handles arranged like A, B or C. The pit is lined with
either stones or bricks, which are heated by a roaring big
fire until hot enough to bake the meat.

THE GOLD DIGGER

Is another bank pit, and one that I have seen used in Montana
by Japanese railroad hands. It is made by digging a hole
in the bank and using shelves either made of stones or old
pieces of iron. Fig. 116 shows the cross section of the Gold

Digger with the stone door in place. Fig. 117 shows a perspective view of the gold digger with the stone door resting at one side.

We next come to the ovens, the first of which is known as

THE FERGUSON CAMP STOVE

It is made by building a rounded hut of stones or sod (Fig. 118), and covering the same with branches over which sod, or clay, or dirt is heaped (Fig. 119). The oven is heated by building the fire inside of it, and when it is very hot and the fire has burned down, the food is placed inside and the opening stopped up so as to retain the heat and thus cook the food.

The Adobe

Is one that the soldiers in Civil War days taught the author to build. The boys in blue generally used an old barrel with the two heads knocked out (Fig. 121). This they either set in the bank or covered with clay (Fig. 120), and in it they built their fires which consumed the barrel but left the baked clay for the sides of the oven. The head of the barrel (Fig. 121A) was saved and used to stop up the front of the oven when baking was being done; a stone or sod was used to cover up the chimney hole. Figs. 122, 123, 124 and 125 show how to make an Adobe by braiding green sticks together and then covering the same with clay, after which it is used in the same manner as the preceding barrel oven.

The Matasiso

Is a camp stove or fire-place, and a form of the so-called Altar Fire-place, the object of which is to save one's back while cooking. The matasiso is built up of stones or sods (Fig. 126) and used like any other campfire.

The Bank Lick

Is a camp stove which the boys of the troop of Boone Scouts, who frequented Bank Lick in old Kentucky, were wont to build and on it to cook the big channel catfish, or little pond bass or other food. The Bank Lick is made of flat stones and is one or two stories high (Figs. 127 and 128). The Boone Scouts flourished in Kenton County, Kentucky, fifty odd years ago.

The Altar Fire-place

Is built of logs (Fig. 132), of stones, of sod, or of logs filled with sods or stone (Fig. 131), and topped with clay (Figs. 130 and 132). The clay top being wider at one end than the other,

THE ADOBE

on the plan of the well-known campfire (Fig. 129), is made with stones and sometimes used when clay is unobtainable.

THE ALTAR CAMP FIRE-PLACE

The advantage of the altar fire and the **matasiso** is that the cook does not have to get the backache over the fire while he cooks. All of these ovens and fire-places are suitable for more or less permanent camps, but it is not worth while to build these ovens and altar fire-places for quick and short camps.

COOKING WITHOUT POTS, PANS OR STOVES

It is proper and right in treating camp cooking that we should begin with the most primitive methods. For when one

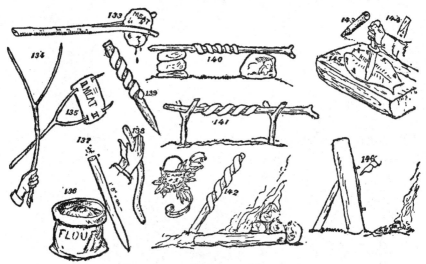

PRIMITIVE COOKING UTENSILS

has no cooking utensils except those fashioned from the material at hand, he must, in order to prepare appetizing food, display a real knowledge of woodcraft.

Therefore, start by spearing the meat on a green twig of sweet birch, or some similar wood, and toast it before the fire or pinch the meat between the split ends of a twig (Fig. 133) or better still

FORK IT

In order to do this select a wand with a fork to it, trim off the prongs of the forks, leaving them rather long (Fig. 134), then sharpen the ends of the prongs and weave them in and out near the edges of the meat (Fig. 135), which is done by drawing the prongs slightly together before impaling the meat on the second prong. The natural spring and elasticity of the branches will stretch the meat nice and flat (Fig. 135), ready to toast in front of the flames, *not over the flame.*

A very thick steak of moose meat or beef may be cooked in this manner. Remember to have fire-dogs and a good back log; there will then be hot coals under the front log and flame against the back log to furnish heat for the meat in front. Turn the meat every few minutes and do not salt it until it is about done. Any sort of meat can be thus cooked; it is a favorite way of toasting bacon among the sportsmen, and I have seen chickens beautifully broiled with no cooking implements but the forked stick. This was done by splitting the chicken open and running the forks through the legs and sides of the fowl.

Pulled Firebread or Twist

Twist is a Boy Scout's name for this sort of bread. The twist is made of dough and rolled between the palms of the hands until it becomes a long thick rope (Fig. 138), then it is wrapped spirally around a dry stick (Fig. 139), or one with bark on it (Fig. 137). The coils should be close together but without touching each other. The stick is now rested in the forks of two uprights, or on two stones in front of the roasting fire (Figs. 140 and 141), or over the hot coals of a pit-fire. The long end of the stick on which the twist is coiled is used for a handle to turn the twist so that it may be nicely browned on all sides, or it may be set upright in front of the flames (Fig. 142).

A Hoe Cake

May be cooked in the same manner that one planks a shad: that is, by plastering it on the flat face of a puncheon or board, split from the trunk of a tree (Fig. 145), or flat clean stone, and propping it up in front of the fire as one would when cooking in a reflecting oven (Fig. 146). When the cake is cooked on one side it can be turned over by using a hunting knife or a little paddle whittled out of a stick for that purpose, and then cooked upon the opposite side. Or a flat stone may be placed over the fire and used as a frying pan (Figs. 116 and 128). I have cooked a large channel catfish in this manner and found that it was unnecessary to skin the fish because, there being no grease, the skin adhered firmly to the hot stone, leaving the white meat flaky and delicate, all ready to be picked out with a jack-knife or with chopsticks, whittled out of twigs.

Meat Hooks

May be made of forked branches (Figs. 151, 152, 153, 154 and 155). Upon this hook meat may be suspended before the fire (Fig. 153) by a piece of twine made from the twisted green bark of a milkweed or some other fibrous plant stalk or tree bark, or a wet string will do if you have one.

How to Dress Small Animals

Dressing in this case really means undressing, taking their coats off and removing their insides. In order to prepare for broiling or baking any of the small fur-bearing animals, make yourself a skinning stick, using for the purpose a forked branch; the forks being about an inch in diameter, make the length of the stick to suit your convenience, that is, long enough to reach between the knees whether you are sitting on a camp stool or squatting on the ground, sharpen the lower end of the stick and thrust it into the ground, then take your coon, possum, squirrel or muskrat, and punch the pointed ends of the forked stick thru the thin place at the point which corresponds to your own heel, just as the stick in Fig. 155 is punched through the thin place behind the heels of the small animals there sketched. Thus hung the animal may be dressed with comfort to the workmen. If one is squatting, the nose of the animal should just clear the ground. First take off the fur coat. To do this you split the skin with a sharp knife, beginning at the center of the throat and cut to the base of the tail, being careful not to cut deep enough to penetrate the inside skin or sack which contains the intestines; when the base of the tail is reached, use your fingers to roll back the skin. If skinning for the pelt, follow directions given later, but do not destroy any skin as the hide is useful for many purposes around camp. After the coat is removed and all the internal organs taken out, remove the scent glands from such animals as have them, and make a cut in the forearms and the meaty parts of the thigh, and cut out the little white things which look like nerves, to be found there. This will prevent the flesh from having a strong or musky taste when it is cooked.

How to Barbecue a Deer, or Sheep

First dress the carcass and then stretch it on a framework of black birch sticks, for this sweet wood imparts no disagreeable odor or taste to the meat.

Next build a big fire at each end of the pit (Fig. 114), not right under the body of the animal, but so arranged that when the melted fat drops from the carcass it will not fall on the hot coals to blaze up and spoil your barbecue. Build big fires with plenty of small sticks so as to make good red hot coals before you put the meat on to cook.

First bake the inside of the barbecued beast, then turn it over and bake the outside. To be well done, an animal the size of a sheep should be cooking at least seven or eight hours over a charcoal fire. Baste the meat with melted bacon fat mixed with any sauce you may have or no sauce at all, for bacon fat itself is good enough for anyone, or use hot salt water.

Of course, it is much better to use charcoal for this purpose, but charcoal is not always handy. One can, however,

MAKE ONE'S OWN CHARCOAL

A day or two ahead of the barbecue day, by building big fires of wood about the thickness of one's wrist. After the fire has been burning briskly for a while, it should be covered up with ashes or dirt and allowed to smoulder all night, and turn the wood into charcoal in place of consuming it

HOW TO MAKE DOUGH

Roll the top of your flour bag back (Fig. 136), then build a cone of flour in the middle of the bag and make a crater in the top of the flour mountain.

In the crater dump a heaping teaspoon—or, to use **Mr.** Vreeland's expression, put in "one and a half heaping tea-spoonfuls of baking powder," to which add a half spoonful of salt; mix these together with the dry flour, and when this is thoroughly done begin to pour water into the crater, a little at a time, mixing the dough as you work by stirring it around inside your miniature volcano. Gradually the flour will slide from the sides into the *lava* of the center, as the water is poured in and care taken to avoid lumps.

Make the dough as soft as may be, not batter but very soft dough, stiff enough, however, to roll between your well-floured hands.

BAKED POTATOES

Put the potatoes with their skins on them on a bed of hot embers two or three inches thick, then cover the potatoes with more hot coals. If this is done properly the spuds will cook slowly, even with the fire burning above them. Don't be a chump and throw the potatoes in the fire where the outer rind will burn to charcoal while the inside remains raw.

MUD COOKING

In preparing a small and tender fish, where possible, the point under the head, where the gills meet, is cut, fingers thrust in and the entrails drawn through this opening; the fish is then washed, cleaned and wrapped in a coating of paper or fallen leaves, before the clay is applied. Place the fish upon a pancake of stiff clay (Fig. 147), fold the clay over the fish (Fig. 148), press the edges together, thus making a clay dumpling (Fig. 149); cook by burying the dumpling in the embers of an ordinary surface fire, or in the embers in a pit-fire (Fig. 150).

A brace of partridges may be beheaded, drawn, washed out thoroughly and stuffed with fine scraps of chopped bacon or pork, mixed with bread crumbs, generously seasoned with salt, pepper and sage, if you have any of the latter. The birds with the feathers on them are then plastered over with clean clay made soft enough to stick to the feathers, the outside is wrapped with stiffer clay and the whole molded into a ball, which is buried deep in the glowing cinders and allowed to remain there for an hour, and at the end of that time the clay will often be almost as hard as pottery and must be broken open with a stick. When the outside clay comes off the feathers will come with it, leaving the dainty white meat of the bird all ready to be devoured.

Woodchucks, raccoons, opossums, porcupines, rabbits had better be barbecued (see Figs. 114, 115 and 155), but squirrels and small creatures may be baked by first removing the insides of the creatures, cleaning them, filling the hollow with bread crumbs, chopped bacon and onions, then closing the opening and plastering the bodies over with stiff clay and baking them in the embers. This seals the meat inside

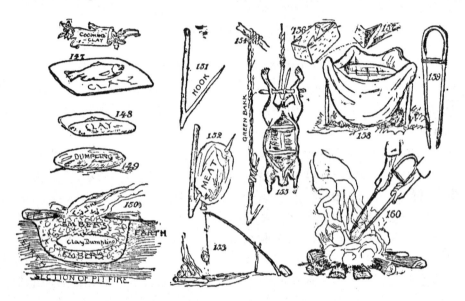

of the mud wrapper and when it is cooked and the brick-like clay broken off, the skin comes off with the broken clay, leaving the juicy meat exposed to view.

To Plank a Fish

Cut off the head of the fish and clean by splitting it through the back, in place of the usual way of splitting up the belly. To salt red meat before you cook it is to make it dry and tough, but the fish should be salted while it is damp with its own juices.

Heat the plank in front of the fire and then spread your fish out flat on the hot puncheon or plank, and with your hunting knife press upon it, make slit holes through the fish (Fig. 145) with the grain of the wood; tack your fish on with wooden pegs cut wedge shape and driven in the slits made by your knife blade (Figs. 143 and 144). Prop the puncheon up in front of a fire which has a good back-log and plenty of hot coals to send out heat (Fig. 146).*

Heating Water

Water may be boiled in a birch bark vessel made by folding up a more or less square piece of bark, bending in the corner (Fig. 157) folds and holding them in place by thorns or slivers (Fig. 156). Or the stomach of a large animal or piece of green hide may be filled with water and the latter made hot by throwing in it hot stones (Fig. 158). Dig a hole in the ground, fit the rawhide in the hole, bringing the edges up so as to overlap the sod, weigh down the edges with stones, fill the hide with water and heat with hot stones. Figs. 159 and 160 show how to make tongs with which to handle the stones.

---

*The best plank is made from the oaks grown on the hammocks of Southern Florida and the peculiar flavor this plank gives to shad has made Planked Shad famous.

CHAPTER VI

CAMP FOOD

HOW TO MAKE ASH CAKE, PONE, CORN DODGERS, FLAPJACKS, JOHNNY-CAKE, BISCUITS AND DOUGHGOD

MAKING DUTCH OVENS

VENISON

BANQUETS IN THE OPEN

HOW TO COOK BEAVER TAIL, PORCUPINES AND MUSKRATS

CAMP STEWS, BRUNSWICK STEWS AND BURGOOS

CHAPTER VI

CAMP FOOD

Parched Corn as Food

When America gave Indian corn to the world she gave it a priceless gift full of condensed pep. Corn in its various forms is a wonderful food power; with a long, narrow buckskin bag of nocake, or rock-a-hominy, as parched cracked corn was called, swung upon his back, an Indian or a white man could traverse the continent independent of game and never suffer hunger. George Washington, George Rodger Clark, Boone, Kenton, Crockett, and Carson all knew the sustaining value of parched corn.

How to Dry Corn

The pioneer farmers in America and many of their descendants up to the present time, dry their Indian corn by the methods the early Americans learned from the Indians. The corn drying season naturally begins with the harvesting of the corn, but it often continues until the first snow falls.

Selecting a number of ears of corn, the husks are pulled back exposing the grain, and then the husks of the several ears are braided together (Fig. 165). These bunches of corn are hung over branches of trees or horizontal poles and left for the winds to dry (Fig. 166).

On account of the danger from corn-eating birds and beasts, these drying poles are usually placed near the kitchen door of the farmhouse, and sometimes in the attic of the old farmhouse, the woodshed or the barn.

Of course, the Indians owned no corn mills, but they used bowl-shaped stones to hold the corn and stone pestles like crudely made potato mashers with which to grind the corn. The writer lately saw numbers of these stone corn-mills in the collection of Doctor Baldwin, of Springfield, Mass.

How to Prepare Corn to Eat

In the southwest much grit from the stone used is unintentionally mixed with the corn, and hence all the elderly Indians' teeth are worn down as if they had been sandpapered.

But the reader can use a wooden bowl and a potato masher with a piece of tin or sheet iron nailed to its bottom with which to crush the corn and make meal without grit. Or he can make a pioneer mill like Figs. 163 or 164, from a log. The pestle or masher in Fig. 164 is of iron.

Sweet Corn

There is a way to preserve corn which a few white people still practice just as they learned it from the Indians. First they dig long, shallow trenches in the ground, fill them with dried roots and small twigs with which they make a hot fire and thus cover the bottom of the ditch with glowing embers. The outer husks of the fresh green corn are then removed and the corn placed in rows side by side on the hot embers (Fig. 167). This practice gave the name of Roasting Ear Season to July and August.

As the husks become scorched the ears are turned over, and when browned on all sides they are deftly tossed out of the ditch by means of a wand or stick used for that purpose.

The burnt husks are now removed and the grains of corn are shelled from the cob with the help of a sharp-edged, fresh water "clam" shell; these shells I have often found in the old camping places of the Indians in the half caves of Pennsylvania.

The corn is then spread out on a clean sheet or on pieces of paper and allowed to dry in the sun. It is "mighty" good food, as any Southern born person will tell you. One can keep a supply of it all winter.

PARCHED FIELD CORN

When I was a little shaver in old Kentucky, the children were very fond of the Southern field corn parched in a frying pan (Fig. 161), and then buttered and salted while it was still hot; we parched field corn, sugar corn and the regular pop corn, but none of us had ever seen cracked corn or corn meal parched and used as food, and I am inclined to think that the old pioneers themselves parched the corn as did their direct descendants in Kentucky, and that said corn was crushed or ground after it had been parched. Be this as it may, we know that our bordermen traveled and fought on a parched corn diet and that Somoset, Massasoit, Pocahontas, Okekankano, Powhatan, all ate corn cakes and that it was either them or the squaws of their tribes who taught bold Captain Smith's people on the southern coast, and the Pilgrims further north, the value of corn as an article of diet. The knowledge of how to make the various kinds of corn bread and the use of corn generally from "roasting-ears" to corn puddings was gained from the American Indians. It was from them we learned how to make the

ASH CAKES

This ancient American food dates back to the fable times which existed before history, when the sun came out of a hole in the eastern sky, climbed up overhead and then dove through a hole in the western sky and disappeared. The sun no more plays such tricks, and although the humming-bird, who once stole the sun, still carries the mark under his chin, he is no longer a humming-birdman but only a little buzzing bird; the ash cake, however, is still an ash cake and is made in almost as primitive a manner now as it was then.

Mix half a teaspoonful of salt with a cup of corn meal, and add to it boiling hot water until the swollen meal may be worked by one's hand into a ball, bury the ball in a nice bed of hot ashes (glowing embers) and leave it there to bake like a potato. Equalling the ash cake in fame and simplicity is

PONE

Pone is made by mixing the meal as described for the ash cake, but molding the mixture in the form of a cone and baking it in an oven.

JOHNNY-CAKE

Is mixed in the same way as the pone or ash cake, but it is not cooked the same, nor is it the same shape; it is more in the form of a very thick pancake. Pat the Johnny-cake into the form of a disk an inch thick and four inches in diameter. Have the frying pan plentifully supplied with *hot* grease and drop the Johnny-cake carefully in the sizzling grease. When the cake is well browned on one side turn it and brown it on the other side. If cooked properly it should be a rich dark brown color and with a crisp crust. Before it is eaten it may be cut open and buttered like a biscuit, or eaten with maple syrup like a hot buckwheat cake. This is the Johnny-cake of my youth, the famous Johnny-cake of Kentucky fifty years ago. Up North I find that any old thing made of corn meal is called a Johnny-cake and that they also call ash-cakes "hoe-cakes," and corn bread "bannocks," at least they call camp corn bread, a bannock. Now since bannocks were known before corn was known, suppose we call it

CAMP CORN BREAD AND CORN DODGERS

In the North they also call this camp corn bread "Johnny-cake," but whatever it is called it is wholesome and nourishing. Take some corn meal and wheat flour and mix them fifty-fifty; in other words, a half pint each; add a teaspoon level full and a teaspoon heaping full of baking powder and about half a teaspoonful of salt; mix these all together, *while dry*, in your pan, then add the water gradually. If you have any milk go fifty-fifty with the water and milk, make the flour as thin as batter, pour it into a reflector pan, or frying pan, prop it up in front of a quick fire; it will be heavy if allowed to cook slowly at the start, but after your cake has risen you may take more time with the cooking. This is a fine corn bread to stick to the ribs. I have eaten it every day for a month at a time and it certainly has the food power in it. When made in form of biscuits it is called "corn dodgers."

Camp Biscuit

Take two cups full of flour and one level teaspoonful and one heaping teaspoonful of baking powder and half a teaspoonful of salt, and mix them together thoroughly while dry. To this you add milk and water, if not milk straight water, mixing it as described for the flapjacks. Make a dough soft but stiff enough to mold with well floured hands, make it into biscuits about half an inch thick, put them into a greased pan, bake them in any one of the ovens already described, or by propping them up in front of the fire. If the biscuits have been well mixed and well baked they will prove to be good biscuits.

The Vreeland Bannock

Fred tells me that he makes this the same as he would biscuits and bakes it in a frying pan. The frying pan is heated and greased before the dough is dropped into it, making a cake about a half inch thick. The frying pan is then placed over the slow fire to give the bannock a chance to rise and harden enough to hold its shape, then the frying pan is propped up with a stick and the bannock browned by reflected heat, it must be cooked slowly and have "a nice brown crust." I have never made bannocks but I have eaten some of Vreeland's, and they are fine.

FLAPJACKS

A fellow who cannot throw a flapjack is sadly lacking in the skill one expects to find in a real woodcrafter. A heavy, greasy flapjack is an abomination, but the real article is a joy to make and a joy to eat.

Put a large tin cupful of flour in the pan, add half a teaspoonful of salt, also one heaping teaspoonful and one level teaspoonful of baking powder; mix the salt and baking powder well with the flour while it is dry. Then build your little mountain or volcano of flour with its miniature crater in the middle, into which pour water little by little; making the lava by mixing the dough as you go. Continue this process until all the flour is batter; the batter should be thin enough to spread out rapidly into the form of a pancake when it is poured into the skillet or frying pan, but not watery.

Grease the frying pan with a greasy rag fastened to the end of a stick or with a piece of bacon rind. Remember that the frying pan only needs enough grease to prevent the cake from sticking to the pan; when one fries potatoes the pan should be plentifully supplied with very hot grease, but flapjacks are not potatoes and too much grease makes the cakes unfit to eat. Do not put too much batter in the pan, either; I tried it once and when I flapped the flapjack the hot batter splattered all over my face, and that batter was even hotter than my remarks.

Pour enough batter into the pan to spread almost but not quite over the bottom; when the bubbles come thickly in the middle and the edges begin to smoke a bit, it is time to flap the flapjack. Do so by loosening the edges with a knife blade, then dip the far side of the pan downward and bring it up quickly, sending the cake somersaulting in the air; catch the cake as it falls batter side down and proceed to cook that side.

The penalty of dropping a flapjack in the fire is to be made to eat it without wiping off the ashes.

Doughgod

First fry some bacon or boil it until it is soft, then chop up the bacon into small pieces quite fine, like hash. Save the grease and set the bacon to one side; now take a pint of flour and half a teaspoon of salt, a spoonful of brown sugar and a heaping spoonful of baking powder and mix them all while they are dry, after which stir in the water as already described until it is in the form of batter; now add the chopped bacon and then mix rapidly with a spoon; pour it into a Dutch oven or a pan and bake; it should be done in thirty-five or forty minutes, according to the condition of the fire.

When your campfire is built upon a hearth made of stones, if you brush the ashes away from the hot stone and place your doughgod upon it, then cover it with a frying pan or some similar vessel, and put the hot cinders on top of the frying pan, you will find that it will bake very nicely and satisfactorily on the hearthstone.

In the old-fashioned open fire-places where our grandparents did their cooking, a Dutch oven was considered essential. The Dutch oven is still used by the guides and cowboys and is of practically the same form as that used by Abraham Lincoln's folks; it consists of a more or less shallow dish of metal, copper, brass or iron, with four metal legs that may be set in the hot cinders. Over that is a metal top which is made so as to cover the bottom dish, and the edges of the cover are turned up all around like a hat with its brim turned up. This is so made to hold the hot cinders which are dumped on top of it, but a

Dutch Oven May be Improvised

From any combination of two metal dishes so made or selected that the large one will fit over the top and snugly overlap the smaller dish, so as not to admit dirt, dust or ashes to the food inside. In this oven bread, biscuits, cakes, pies, stews, bakes, meat, fish, fowl and vegetables may be cooked with delightful results. In camp two frying pans are frequently made to act as a Dutch oven. A Dutch oven is sometimes used in a bean hole (Fig. 106). First build a fire, using sufficient small wood, chips and dry roots to make cinders enough with which to fill your bean hole. While the fire is doing its work let the cook prepare to cook

The Sourdough's Joy

Slice bacon as thin as possible and place a layer over the bottom and around the sides of the Dutch oven like a pie-crust. Slice venison, moose meat or bear steak, or plain beef, medium thin and put in to the depth of $2\frac{1}{2}$ inches, salting each layer. Chop a large onion and sprinkle it over the top, cover with another layer of bacon and one pint of water and put on the lid. Fill the hole half full of hot embers, place the Dutch oven in the center and fill the space surrounding the oven full of embers. Cover all with about 6 inches of dirt, then roll yourself up in your blanket and shut your eyes— your breakfast will cook while you sleep and be piping hot when you dig for it in the morning.

The bean hole is far from a modern invention and the dried droppings of animals, like "buffalo chips," were used for fuel away back in Bible times; in ancient Palestine they stewed their meat in a pot set in a hole filled in with stones over which burned a fire of "chips" gathered where the flocks pastured.

When the wood is of such a nature that it is difficult to obtain a bed of live coals for toasting, meat may, in a pinch, be cooked upon a clean flat stone (Figs. 116, 117 and 128). Be certain that the stone is a dry one, otherwise the heat may burst it. If satisfied that it is dry, heat it good and hot and spread your thick slice of venison, moose, bear or sheep or even beef upon the very hot stone; leave it there about twenty minutes and allow it to singe, sizzle and burn on one side, then turn it over and burn the other side until the charred part is one-quarter or even a half inch deep. Now remove the meat and with your hunting knife scrape away all the charred meat, season it and toast some bacon or pork on a forked stick and, after scoring the steak deeply and putting the pork or bacon in the cuts, the meat is ready to serve to your hungry self and camp mates.

How to Cook Venison

If you want to know how real wild meat tastes, drop a sleek buck with a shot just over the shoulder—no good sportsman will shoot a doe—dress the deer and let it hang for several days; that is, if you wish tender meat. Cut a steak two inches thick and fry some bacon, after which put the steak in the frying pan with the bacon on top of it, and a cover on the frying pan. When one side is cooked, turn the meat over and again put the bacon on top, replace the cover and let that side cook. Serve on a hot plate and give thanks that you are in the open, have a good appetite and you are privileged to partake of a dish too good for any old king. The gravy, oh my word! the recollection of it makes me hungry! I have eaten moose meat three times a day for weeks at a time, when it was cooked as described, without losing my desire for more.

PERDIX AU CHOUX

Is a great dish in Canada; the bird is cooked this way: Chop cabbage fine and highly spice it, then stuff the bird with the cabbage and nicely cover the partridge or grouse with many thin slices of bacon, and put bacon also in the baking pan. When this is well baked and well basted a more delicious game dinner you will never eat. Try it; it is an old French way of cooking the partridge or pheasant.

When you need a real warm fire for cooking, do not forget that dry roots make an intensely hot fire with no smoke; look for them in driftwood piles, as they are sure to be there; they are light as a cork and porous as a sponge, and burn like coke.

No one with truth may say that he is a real woodcrafter unless he is a good camp cook. At the same time it is an error to think that the outdoor men live to eat like the trencher men of old England, or the degenerate epicures of ancient Rome. Neither are the outdoor men in sympathy with the Spartans or Lacedemonians and none of them would willingly partake of the historic and disgusting black broth of Lacedemonia. Woodcrafters are really more in sympathy with cultured Athenians who strove to make their banquets attractive with interesting talk, inspiring and patriotic odes and delightful recitations by poets and philosophers. As a campfire man would say: "That's me all over, Mable" and he might add that like all good things on this earth

8

Banquets

Originated in the open. The word itself is from the French and Spanish and means a small bench, a little seat, and when spelled banqueta, means a three-legged stool. It has reference to sitting while eating instead of taking refreshments in "stand up" fashion. The most enjoyable banquets in the author's experience are those partaken in the wilderness, and prominent among the wildwood dishes is the

Lumberman's Baked Beans

Wash the beans first, then half fill a pail with them, put them over the fire and parboil them until their skins are ready to come off; they are now ready for the pot. But before putting them in there, peel an onion and slice it, placing the slices in the bottom of the bean pot. Now pour half of the beans over the onions and on top of them spread the slices of another onion. Take some salt pork and cut it into square pieces and place the hunks of pork over the onions, thus making a layer of onions and pork on top of the beans. Over this pour the remainder of the beans, cover the top of the beans with molasses, on the top of the molasses put some more hunks of pork, put in enough water to barely cover the beans. Over the top of all of it spread a piece of birch bark, then force the cover down good and tight.

Meanwhile a fire should have been built in the bean hole (Fig. 105). When the fire of birch has been burnt to hot cinders, the cinders must be shoveled out and the bean pot put into the hole, after which pack the cinders around the bean pot and cover the whole thing with the dead ashes, or as the lumbermen call them, the black ashes.

If the beans are put into the bean hole late in the afternoon and allowed to remain there all night, they will be done to a turn for breakfast; the next morning they will be wholesome, juicy and sweet, browned on top and delicious.

A bean hole is not absolutely necessary for a small pot of beans. I have cooked them in the wilderness by placing the pot on the ground in the middle of the place where the fire had been burning, then heaping the hot ashes and cinders over the bean pot until it made a little hill there, which I covered with the black ashes and left until morning. I tried the same experiment on the open hearth to my studio and it was a wonderful success.

The Etiquette of the Woods

Requires that when a porcupine has been killed it be immediately thrown into the fire, there to remain until all the quills have been singed off of the aggressive hide, after which it may be skinned with no danger to the workmen and with no danger to the other campers from the wicked barbed quills, which otherwise might be waiting for them just where they wished to seat themselves.

This may sound funny, but I have experimented, unintentionally, by seating myself upon a porcupine quill. I can assure the reader that there is nothing humorous in the experience to the victim, however funny it may appear to those who look on.

After thoroughly singeing the porcupine you roll it in the grass to make certain that the burnt quills are rubbed off its skin, then with a sharp knife slit him up the middle of the belly from the tail to the throat, pull the skin carefully back and peel it off. When you come to the feet cut them off. Broiled porcupine is the Thanksgiving turkey of the Alaskan and British Columbia Indian, but unless it has been boiled in two or three waters the taste does not suit white men.

Porcupine Wilderness Method

After it has been parboiled, suspend the porcupine by its forelegs in front of a good roasting fire, or over a bed of hot coals, and if well seasoned it will be as good meat as can be found in the wilderness. The tail particularly is very meaty and is most savory; like beef tongue it is filled with fine bits of fat. Split the tail and take out the bone, then roast the meaty part.

Porcupine stuffed with onions and roasted on a spit before the fire is good, but to get the perfection of cooking it really should be cooked in a Dutch oven, or a closed kettle or an improvised airtight oven of some sort and baked in a bean hole, or baked by being buried deep under a heap of cinders and covered with ashes. Two iron pans that will fit together, that is, one that is a trifle larger than the other so that the smaller one may be pushed down into it to some extent, will answer all the purposes of the Dutch oven. Also two frying pans arranged in the same manner.

Always remember that after the porcupine is skinned, dressed and cleaned, it should be *put in a pot and parboiled*, changing the water once or twice, after which it may be cooked in any way which appeals to the camper. The

North Method

Is to place it in the Dutch oven with a few hunks of fat pork; let the porcupine itself rest upon some hard-tack, hard biscuit or stale bread of any kind, which has been slightly softened with water.

On top of the porcupine lay a nice slice or two of fat pork and place another layer of soaked hard biscuit or hard-tack on the pork, put it in a Dutch oven and place the Dutch oven on the hot coals, put a cover on the Dutch oven and heap the living coals over the top of it and the ashes atop of that; let it bake slowly until the flesh parts from the bones. Thus cooked it will taste something like veal with a suggestion of sucking pig. The tail of the porcupine, like the

TAIL OF THE BEAVER

Is considered a special delicacy. Many of the old wilderness men hang the flat trowel-like tails of the beaver for a day or two in the chimney of their shack to allow the oily matter to exude from it, and thus take away the otherwise strong taste; others parboil it as advocated for porcupine meat, after which the tail may be roasted or baked and the rough skin removed before eating.

BEAVER TAIL SOUP

Is made by stewing the tails with what other ingredients one may have in camp; all such dishes should be allowed to simmer for a long while in place of boiling rapidly.

A man who was hunting in North Michigan said, "Although I am a Marylander, and an Eastern Shore one at that, and consequently know what good things to eat are, I want to tell you that I'll have to take off my hat to the lumber camp cook as the discoverer, fabricator and dispenser of a dish that knocks the Eastern Shore cuisine silly. And that dish is beaver-tail soup. When the beaver was brought into camp the camp cook went nearly wild, and so did the lumbermen when they heard the news, and all because they were pining for beaver-tail soup.

"The cook took that broad appendage of the beaver, mailed like an armadillo, took from it the underlying bone and meat and from it made such a soup as never came from any other stock, at the beck of the most expert and scientific chef that ever put a kettle on."

MUSKRAT

Is valuable also for his flesh. Its name and rat-like appearance have created a prejudice against it as a food, but thousands of persons eat it without compunction. For those to whom the name is a stumbling-block the euphemism "marsh rabbit" has been invented, and under this name the muskrat is sold even in the Wilmington market and served on the tables of white country folk. In Delaware, especially, the muskrat is ranked as a delicacy, and personally the author ranks this rodent with the rabbit as an article of food.

At Dover the writer has had it served at the hotel under its own name; the dish was "muskrats and toast." For the benefit of those who revolt at the muskrat as food, it is well to state that it is one of the cleanest of all creatures, that it carefully washes all its own food and in every way conducts itself so as to recommend its flesh even to the most fastidious. As a matter of fact the flesh of the muskrat, though dark, is tender and exceedingly sweet. Stewed like rabbit it looks and tastes like rabbit, save that it lacks a certain gamy flavor that some uneducated persons find an unpleasant characteristic of the latter. But to the writer's way of thinking, while the muskrat is good to eat, there are many things much better; the point is, however, that everything which tastes good and is not indigestible is good to eat no matter what its name may be.

THE BURGOO

Of all the camp stews and hunters' stews of various names and flavors, the Kentucky burgoo heads the list; not only is it distinguished for its intrinsic qualities, its food value and delicious flavor, its romance and picturesque accompaniment, but also because of the illustrious people whose names are linked in Kentucky history with the burgoo. One such feast, given some time between 1840 and 1850, was attended by Governor Owlsley (old stone-hammer), Governor Metcalf, Governor Bob Letcher, Governor Moorhead, General George Crittenton, General John Crittenton, General Tom Crittenton, James H. Beard, and other distinguished men.

All Kentuckians will vow they understand the true meaning of the word "burgoo." But an article in the Insurance Field says, "It is derived from the low Latin burgus, fortified (as a town) and goo-goo, very good." Hence the word, "burgoo," something very good, fortified with other good things, as will be found in "Carey's Dictionary of Double Derivations": "Burgoo is literally a soup composed of many vegetables and meats delectably fused together in an enormous caldron, over which, at the exact moment, a rabbit's foot at the end of a yarn string is properly waved by a colored preacher, whose salary has been paid to date. These are the good omens by which the burgoo is fortified."

How to Make the Burgoo

Anything from an ordinary pail to one or many big caldrons, according to the number of guests expected at the camp, will serve as vessels in which to serve the burgoo. The excellence of the burgoo depends more upon the manner of cooking and seasoning it than it does on the material used in its decoction.

To-day the burgoo is composed of meat from domestic beasts and barnyard fowls with vegetables from the garden, but originally it was made from the wild things in the woods, bear, buffalo, venison, wild turkey, quails, squirrels and all the splendid game animals that once roamed through Kentucky.

As this book is for woodcrafters we will take it for granted that we are in the woods, that we have some venison, moose, bear meat, rocky mountain goat, big horn, rabbit, ruffed grouse, or some good substitutes. It would be a rare occasion indeed when we would really have these things. If, for instance, we have a good string of grouse we will take their legs and wings and necks for the burgoo and save their breasts for a broil, and if we have not many grouse we will put in a whole bird or two. We will treat the rabbits the same way, saving the body with the tenderloin for broiling. When cleaned and dressed the meat of a turtle or two adds a delicious flavor to the burgoo; frogs legs are also good, with the other meat.

Cut all the meat up into pieces which will correspond, roughly speaking, to inch cubes; do not throw away the bones; put them in also. Now then, if you were wise enough when you were outfitting for the trip to secure some of the ill-smelling but palatable dried vegetables, they will add immensely to the flavor of your burgoo. Put all the material in the kettle, that is, unless you are using beans and potatoes as vegetables; if so, the meats had better be well cooked first, because the beans and potatoes have a tendency to go to the bottom, and by scorching spoil the broth.

Fill your kettle, caldron or pot half full of water and hang it over the fire; while it is making ready to boil get busy with your vegetables, preparing them for the stew. Peel the dry outer skin off your onions and halve them, or quarter them, according to their size; scrape your carrots and slice them into little disks, each about the size of a quarter, peel your potatoes and cut them up into pieces about the size of the meat, and when the caldron is boiling dump in the vegetables. The vegetables will temporarily cool the water, which should not be allowed to again boil, but should be put over a slow fire and where it will simmer. When the stew is almost done add the salt and other seasonings. There should always be enough water to cover the vegetables. Canned tomatoes will add to the flavor of your broth. In a real burgoo we put no thickening like meal, rice or other material of similar nature, because the broth is strained and served clear. Also no sweet vegetables like beets.

When the burgoo is done dip it out and drink it from tin cups. Of course, if this is a picnic burgoo, you add olive juice to the stew, while it is cooking, and then place a sliced lemon and an olive in each cup and pour the hot strained liquid into the cups.

The burgoo and the barbecue belong to that era when food was plenty, feasts were generous and appetites good. These historic feasts still exist in what is left of the open country and rich farming districts, particularly in Kentucky and Virginia. In Kentucky in the olden times the gentlemen were wont to go out in the morning and do the hunting, while the negroes were keeping the caldrons boiling with the pork and other foundation material in them. After the gentlemen returned and the game was put into the caldron, the guests began to arrive and the stew was served late in the afternoon; each guest was supposed to come supplied with a tin cup and a spoon, the latter made of a fresh water mussel shell with a split stick for a handle. Thus provided they all sat round and partook of as many helps as their hunger demanded.

Since we have given Kentucky's celebrated dish, we will add "Ole Virginny's" favorite dish, which has been named after the county where it originated.

The Brunswick Stew

"Take two large squirrels, one quart of tomatoes, peeled and sliced, if fresh; one pint of lima beans or butter beans, two teaspoonfuls of white sugar, one minced onion, six potatoes, six ears of corn scraped from the cob, or a can of sweet corn, half a pound of butter, half a pound of salt pork, one teaspoonful of salt, three level teaspoonfuls of pepper and a gallon of water. Cut the squirrels up as for fricassee, add salt and water and boil five minutes. Then put in the onion, beans, corn, pork, potatoes and pepper, and when boiling again add the squirrel.

"Cover closely and stew two hours, then add the tomato mixed with the sugar and stew an hour longer. Ten minutes before removing from the fire cut the butter into pieces the size of English walnuts, roll in flour and add to the stew. Boil up again, adding more salt and pepper if required."

The above is a receipt sent in to us, and I would give credit for it if I knew from whence it came. I do know that it sounds good, and from my experience with other similar dishes, it will taste good.

I am not writing a cook book but only attempting to start the novice on his way as a camp chef, and if he succeeds in cooking in the open the dishes here described, he need not fear to tackle any culinary problem which conditions may make it necessary for him to solve.

CHAPTER VII

PACKING HORSES

CHAPTER VII

PACKING HORSES

If one is going on a real camping excursion where one will need pack horses, one should, by all means, familiarize oneself with the proper method of packing a pack horse. This can be done in one's own cellar, attic or woodshed and without hiring a horse or keeping one for the purpose. The horse will be expensive enough when one needs it on the trail.

The drill in packing a horse should be taught in all scout camps, and all girl camps and all Y. M. C. A. camps, and all training camps; in fact, everywhere where anybody goes outdoors at all, or where anybody pretends to go outdoors; and after the tenderfeet have learned how to pack then it is the proper time to learn what to pack; consequently we put packing before outfitting, not the cart, but the pack before the horse, so to speak.

When the Boy Scout Movement started in America it had the good aggressive American motto, "BE SURE YOU'RE RIGHT, THEN GO AHEAD," which was borrowed from that delightful old buckskin man, Davy Crockett.

A few years later, when the scout idea was taken up in England, the English changed the American motto to "BE PREPARED;" because the English Boy Scout promoter was a military man himself and saw the necessity of preparedness by Great Britain, which has since become apparent to us all.

And in order to be prepared to pack a horse, we must first be sure we are right, then "go ahead" and practice packing at home.

One of the most useful things to the outdoor person is a

PACK HORSE

All of us do not own a horse, but there is not a reader of this book so poor that he cannot own the horse shown by Fig. 174.

There are but few people in the United States who cannot honestly come into possession of a barrel with which to build a pack horse or on which to practice throwing the diamond hitch. They can also find, somewhere, some pieces of board with which to make the legs of the horse, its neck and head.

Fig. 168 shows the neck-board, and the dotted lines show where to saw the head to get the right angle for the head and ears, with which the horse may hear. Fig. 169 shows the head-board, and the dotted line shows how to saw off one corner to give the proper shape to this Arabian steed's intelligent head-piece.

Fig. 170 shows how to nail the head on the neck. The nails may be procured by knocking them out of old boards; at least that is the way the writer supplied himself with nails. He does not remember ever asking his parents for money with which to buy nails, but if it is different nowadays, and if you do not feel economically inclined, and have the money, go to the shop and buy them. Also, under such circumstances, go to the lumber yard and purchase your boards.

Fig. 171 shows how to nail two cleats on the neck, and Fig. 172 shows how to nail these cleats onto the head of the barrel. If you find the barrel head so tough and elastic that a nail cannot be easily hammered in, use a gimlet and bore holes into the cleats and into the barrel head, and then fasten the cleats on with screws.

The tail of the nag is made out of an old piece of frayed rope (Fig. 173), with a knot tied in one end to prevent the tail from pulling out when it is pulled through a hole in the other end of the barrel (Fig. 173). The legs of the horse are made like those of a carpenter's wooden horse, of bits of plank or boards braced under the barrel by cross-pieces (Fig. 174).

Now you have a splendid horse! "One that will stand without hitching." It is kind and warranted not to buck, bite or kick, but nevertheless, when you are packing him remember that you are doing it in order to drill yourself to pack a real live horse, a horse that may really buck, bite and kick.

There are a lot of words in the English language not to be found in the dictionary. I remember a few years ago when one could not find "undershirt" or "catboat" in the dictionary. But in the dictionaries of to-day you will even find "aparejo" and "latigo," although neither of these words was in the dictionaries of yesterday.

MAKE YOUR OWN APAREJO

Make your own aparejo of anything you can find. The real ones are made of leather, but at the present time, 1920, leather is very expensive. We can, however, no doubt secure some builders' paper, tar paper, stiff wrapping paper, a piece of old oilcloth, which, by the way, would be more like leather than anything else, and cover these things with a piece of tent cloth, a piece of carpet, or even burlap. The oilcloth inside will stiffen the aparejo. At the bottom edge of it we can lash a couple of sticks (Fig. 175), or if we want to do it in a real workmanlike manner, we can sew on a couple of leather shoes, made out of old shoe leather or new leather if we can secure it, and then slip a nice hickory stick through the shoes, as shown in the diagram (Fig. 176).

The aparejo is to throw over the horse's back as in Fig. 178, but in order to fasten it on the back we must have a latigo which is the real wild and woolly name for the rope attached to a cincha strap (Fig. 177). But when you are talking about packing the pack horses call it "cinch," and spell it "cincha." Make your cincha of a piece of canvas, and in one end fasten a hook—a big strong picture hook will do; Fig. 177½ shows a cinch hook made of an oak elbow invented by Stewart Edward White, and in the other end an iron ring; to the iron ring fasten the lash rope (Fig. 177).

For the real horse and outfit one will need an aparejo,

a pack blanket, a lash rope with a cincha, a sling rope, a blind for the horse, and a pack cover. But here again do not call it a pack cover, for that will at once stamp you as a tenderfoot. Assume the superior air of a real plainsman and speak of it as a "manta." The aparejo and pack saddle are inventions of the Arabians away back in the eighth century. When the Moors from Africa overran Spain, these picturesque marauders brought with them pack mules, pack saddles, and aparejos. When General Cortez and Pizarro carried the torch and sword through Mexico in their search for gold, they brought with them pack animals, pack saddles, aparejos, latigos, and all that sort of thing with which to pack their loot.

When the forty-niners went to California in search of gold they found that the Arabian Moorish-Spanish-Mexican method of packing animals was perfectly adapted to their purposes and they used to pack animals, the aparejos, the latigos, and all the other kinds of gos. The lash rope for a real pack horse should be of the best Manila $\frac{1}{2}$ inch or $\frac{5}{8}$ inch, and forty feet long; a much shorter one will answer for the wooden horse.

Even Boys Can Throw the Hitch

Back in 1879, Captain A. B. Wood, United States Army, introduced a knowledge of the proper use of the pack saddle and the mysteries of the diamond hitch into the United States Army. The Fourth Cavalry, United States Army, was the first to become expert with the diamond hitch and taught it to the others; but recently a military magazine has asked permission, and has used the author's diagrams, to explain to the Cavalry men how this famous hitch is thrown.

It stands to reason that in order to pack one horse one

9

must have some packs. But these are the easiest things imaginable to secure. A couple of old potato or flour bags, stuffed with anything that is handy—hay, grass, leaves, rags or paper—but stuffed tight (Fig. 179), will do for our load.

When packing a horse, except with such hitches as the "one man hitch," it requires two men or boys to "throw" the hitch. The first one is known as the head packer, and the

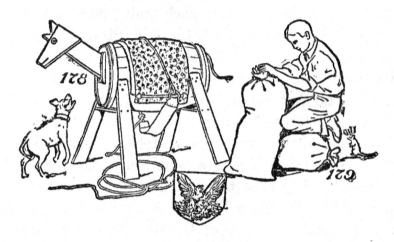

other as the second packer. Remember that the left-hand side of the horse is the nigh side. The head packer stands on the nigh side of the horse and he takes the coiled lash rope in the left hand and lets the coils fall astern of the pack animal (Fig. 180); with the right hand he takes hold of the rope about three or four feet from the cincha (Fig. 180) and hands the hook end under the animal to the second packer, who stands on the right-hand side of the horse (Fig. 180). The right hand of the head packer, with the palm upwards, so holds the rope that the loop will fall across his forearm; the left hand with the palm downward holds the rope about half way between the loop that goes over the forearm and the loop that lies along the back of the pack animal (Fig. 181). The head packer now throws the loop from his forearm across

the pack on the back of the animal, allowing the left hand to fall naturally on the neck of the animal. The second packer now runs the rope through the hook and pulls up the cincha end until the hook is near the lower edge of the off side of the aparejo (Fig. 183).

The head packer next grasps the rope A (Fig. 185) and tucks a loop from the rear to the front under the part marked B (Figs. 185 and 186), over the inner side pack (Figs. 184 and 187). Next the second packer passes the loose end of the rope under the part marked D (Fig. 187), and throws it on the nigh (left) side of the pack animals.

The head packer now draws the tucked loop forward and tucks it under the corners and the lower edge of the nigh side of the aparejo (Fig. 188), then holds it taut from the rear corner, and the second packer takes hold of the rope at E (Fig. 189) with his left hand, and at F (Fig. 187) with his right hand. He passes the rope under the corners and lower edge of the off side of the aparejo (G, H, Fig. 189, and G, H, Fig. 191). The second packer now takes the blind off his pack animal and is supposed to lead it forward a few steps while the head packer examines the load from the rear to see if it is properly adjusted.

Then the blind is again put upon the animal for the final tightening of the rope. While the second packer is pulling the parts taut, the head packer takes up the slack and keeps the pack steady. The tightening should be done in such a manner as not to shake the pack out of balance or position, (Figs. 188 and 190).

The second (or off side) packer grasps the lash rope above the hook, and puts his knee against the stern corner of the aparejo, left-hand group (Fig. 188). The head packer takes hold with his right hand of the same part of the rope where it comes from the pack on the inner side, and with the left hand at J (Fig. 189), and his right shoulder against the cargo to steady it, he gives the command "PULL!" Without jerks, but with steady pulls, the second packer now tightens the

W IS A REAL CINCHA AND LATIGO
X IS A REAL SAWBUCK SADDLE WITH
ALFORJAS ATTACHED

rope, taking care not to let it slip back through the hook. He gives the loose part to the head packer, who takes up the slack by steady pulls.

When the second packer is satisfied that it is all right he cries, "Enough!" The head packer then holds steady with his right hand and slips the other hand down to where the rope passes over the front edge of the aparejo. There he holds steady; his right hand then takes hold of the continuation of the rope at the back corner of the pad and pulls tight. Placing his right knee against the rear corner of the pad he pulls hard with both hands until the rope is well home, left-hand group (Fig. 188).

The second packer now takes up the slack by grasping the rope with both hands, E (Fig. 189).

The head packer steps to the front to steady the pack. The second packer pulls taut the parts on his side, taking up the slack. This draws the part of the lash rope K, K (Fig. 189), well back at middle of the pack, giving the center hitch the diamond shape from which the name is derived, X (Fig. 191). He then, with the left hand at the rear corner H, pulls taut and holds solid, while with the right hand in front of G, he takes up slack. Next with both hands at the front corner and with his knee against it (Fig. 188), the second packer pulls taut, the head packer at the same time taking up the slack on his side and then pulls steady, drawing the part L, L (Fig. 189), of the rope leading from the hook well forward at the middle of the pack, finishing off the diamond at X. He then carries the loose end under the corners and ends of the aparejo, and draws that taut and ties the end fast by a half hitch near the cincha end of the lash rope.

After passing under the corners, if the rope is long enough to reach over the load, it can then be passed over and made fast on the off side by tying around both parts of the lash rope above the hook and by drawing them well together (Fig. 191).

Alongside of Fig. 190 are a series of sketches showing how to lash and cinch two parcels or bags together; one bag is made black so that its position can better be understood. In other words, it makes it easier to follow the different hitches.

Learn to pack at home and you will not lose your packs on the trail.

In following these instructions, whenever in doubt forget the perspective views and keep in mind Figures 181, 183, 185, 187, 189 and 191, which tell the whole story. The perspective views are principally to show the relative position of the packers; the position of the rope can best be seen by looking on top of the pack.

In packing a live horse you will learn by practice not to pull in such a way as to cause the horse to step on your feet; you will also learn that a live horse will not stand as still as a wooden horse, but when you have learned to pack a wooden horse quickly and well, it will only take you a short time to become expert with a live horse.

The Squaw Hitches

These are useful when one has no one to help in packing the animal, and when one has no pack saddle like Fig. 200. With this squaw hitch you must throw your burden across the back of the horse, over the pad made by a blanket (Fig.

192), then put a loop over the end M, see X (Fig. 192), and another one over the end N, see Y (Fig. 192). At the end of the lash rope Z make a loop; now pass that loop down under the horse's belly and through Y (Fig. 193), bring the end Z back again over the horse's back, also pass the end T down through X, and bring it back over the horse's back, also pass the end Z down through Y, and bring it back over the horse's

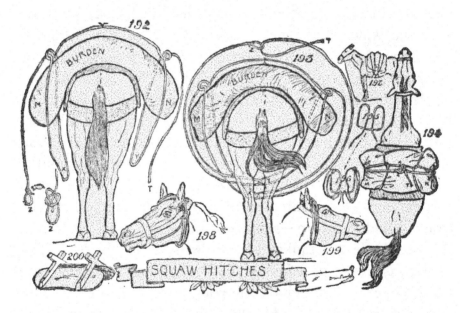

SQUAW HITCHES

back, pass T through Z (Fig. 193), cinch tight and fasten on top of pack (Fig. 194). Fig. 195 shows another throw in another squaw hitch. Fig. 196 shows the next position. Fig. 197 shows the thing made fast.

Anyone who travels with pack horses should know how to arrange the lead rope in a manner so that it may be quickly and easily loosened, and at the same time be out of the way, so that the horse will not get his foot over it when climbing or descending steep places, which often happens when the lead rope is fastened to the pack in the usual manner. If you will take the rope and wind it loosely around the horse's neck, behind his left ear and in front of his right ear (Figs. 198 and 199), then tuck the end under the strands, as shown in Fig. 198, the thing may be undone in an instant, and in the meantime the rope is out of the way where it will not bother either the man or the horse.

Practise all this on the wooden horse, then it will come natural when the time comes to handle a real horse. The manner of looping up the lead rope, just described, I learned from the explorers of the Mt. McKinley expedition, who had many occasions to test the best, as well as the worst methods of packing and arranging their duffel. There are a number of other hitches, some given by Stewart Edward White, in *Outing*, called the Miner's Hitch, the Lone Packer's Hitch, but possibly we have given the reader enough to start him on his way; remember for the pack horse the necessary outfit is a horse blanket, the cincha and lash rope, the sling rope, the lead rope, the manta, which is a cover for the pack, sometimes called the tarp—short for tarpaulin, and the blind, but as a rule a handkerchief is used for a blinder. The aparejo is a sort of a leather mattress which goes over the horse's back and on which the pack rests, but you will find all about that when you hit the trail with a pack train. The alforjas is a Spanish name for the saddle-bags used on a pack horse. When the reader knows how to pack his horse, knows all the Spanish names for the pack saddle and all that sort of thing, there may come a time when he will have a horse which needs to be hitched at night, and it may happen he must needs

Hitch the Horse

On some trail where there are no trees, sticks, or even stones; but if he is a good woodcrafter and plainsman, with his hunting knife he will proceed to dig as narrow and deep a hole as

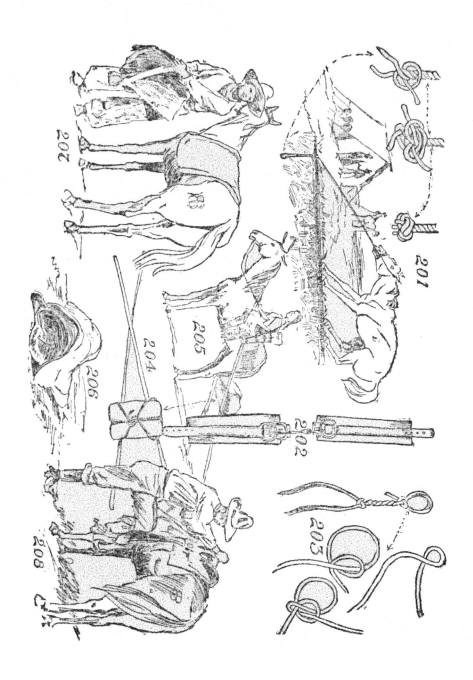

possible in the earth, then he will tie a knot in the end of the picket rope and drop the knot to the bottom of the hole (Fig. 201) (the picket rope in reality should be one-half inch rope, fifty feet long); the only way to get that knot out of the hole is to stand directly over the opening and pull the knot up perpendicularly. It will never occur to the horse to shorten the line by taking hold of it with his teeth, so that it may stand over the hole and pull up the knot, consequently the animal will be as securely hitched as if tied to a post.

Hobbles

For the front legs may be purchased at any outfitter's (Fig. 202), or home-made from unravelled rope (Fig. 203). Make a loop from a strand from a large rope and then fasten it round one leg, as in diagram; after that twist the rope to make the connections between the two loops, tie another knot to prevent the rope from untwisting, then tie the two ends around the leg of the horse (Fig. 203); the unravelled rope is soft and will not chafe the horse's leg.

Travois

Figs. 204 and 205 show the famous Indian mode of packing by travois.

How to Throw a Saddle Down

General Miles once told the author that the handsomest man he had ever seen came dashing into their camp in a cloud of alkali dust; having ridden right through bands of hostile Indians which surrounded the camp, he dismounted, took off his saddle and threw it on the ground, put the bridle bit, girth, etc., inside the saddle, put the saddle-cloth over it, then he calmly stretched himself out in front of the campfire. "That man," said General Miles, "was Bill Cody, Buffalo Bill!"

When Cody put the saddle on the ground he placed it on its side (Fig. 206); in placing the saddle in this position it preserves the curve of the skirts, and thus the form of the saddle is not destroyed and the reins and the stirrup straps are protected; at the same time the saddle makes a good pillow, and if it should rain at night the saddle blanket is the only thing, besides the rider, which gets a ducking, unless the latter has a good waterproof sleeping-bag.

How to Throw a Saddle on a Horse

So manage the saddle that with one swing it will 'light on the horse's back with the pummel towards the horse's head (Fig. 207). Grasp with your right hand the horn of the saddle, and as you swing the saddle on the horse with a graceful sweep, use your left hand to push the further skirt outward and thus prevent it from doubling up on the horse's back. Be careful to throw the girth far enough so that it will hang down so as to be easily reached under the horse. I once had an English farm hand who put a western saddle on a horse with the *pummel towards the tail*, and was very indignant when I told him that a pummel should face the bow of a craft; he told me he knew more about horses than I did, which is possibly true, as I am not a horseman; he also said that in the "hold country" he used to ride to "the 'ounds," all of which goes to prove customs are different in different countries. Here we put the pummel of the saddle towards the horse's head; we won't argue about it; we may be wrong, but it is a matter of custom, and right or wrong is the rule the reader must follow in America, even though the reader may have ridden to the "'ounds" while abroad. Do not misunderstand me, some of the best horsemen in the world are English, but this fellow was not one of them.

How to Mount a Western Horse

Years ago when the rider was in Montana on Howard Eaton's Ranch, near the celebrated ranch of Theodore Roosevelt, he had his first experience with Western horses, and being sensitive and standing in great terror of being called a tenderfoot, he shyly watched the others mount before he attempted to do so himself. Each one of these plainsmen, he noticed, took the reins in his left hand while standing on the left-hand side of the horse; then holding the reins over the shoulders of the horse he grasped the mane with the same hand, and put his left foot into the stirrup; but to put the left foot in the stirrup he turned the stirrup around so that he could mount while facing the horse's tail, then he grabbed hold of the pummel with his right hand and swung into the saddle as the horse started.

That looked easy; the writer also noticed that just before the others struck the saddle they gave a whoop, so without showing any hesitation the author walked up to his cayuse, took the reins confidently in his left hand, using care to stand on the left-hand side of the horse; then he placed the left hand with the reins between the shoulders of the horse and grabbed the mane, then he turned the stirrup around, turned his back to the horse's head, put his left foot in the stirrup and gave a yell.

On sober afterthought he decided that he gave that yell too soon; the horse almost went out from under him, or at least so it seemed to him, or maybe the sensation would be better described to say that it appeared to him as if he went a mile over the prairie with his right leg waving in the air like a one-winged aeroplane, before he finally settled down into the saddle.

But this could not have been really true, because everybody applauded and the writer was at once accepted by the crowd without question as a thoroughbred Sourdough. Possibly they may have thought he was feeling good and just doing some stunts.

It may interest the reader to state that the author did his best to live up to the first impression he had made, but *he did not go riding the next day,* there were some books he thought necessary to read; he discovered, however, that even lounging was not without some discomfort; for instance, he could not cross his knees without helping one leg over with both his hands; in fact, he could find no muscle in his body that could be moved without considerable exertion and pain.

But this is the point of the story: Had the author tried to mount that cayuse in any other way he would have been left sprawling on the prairie. The truth is that if you mount properly when the horse starts, even if he begins to buck and pitch, the action will tend to throw you into the saddle, **not** out of it.

Caution

When you approach a horse *which has a brand* on it, always approach from the left-hand side, because practically all the Western horses have brands on them, and you can, as a rule, count on a branded horse being from the West, with the hale and hearty habits of the West, which to be appreciated must be understood. If you want to make a real cayuse out of your wooden horse, brand it and any cowboy who then sees it will take off his hat.

CHAPTER VIII

THE USE OF DOGS. MAN PACKING

CHAPTER VIII

THE USE OF DOGS. MAN PACKING

THERE is no good reason why every hiker should not be accompanied by

A HIKING DOG

For if there is anything a dog does love better than its own soul it is to hike with its master, and every normal boy and girl, and every normal man and woman, loves the company of a good dog. When they do not love it the fault is not with the dog but with them; there is something wrong with them that the outdoor world alone will cure.

But if a dog is going to enjoy the pleasure of a hike with you, if it is a good square dog it should be willing to also share the hardships of the hike with you, and to help carry the burdens on the trail. Any sort of a dog can be trained as

A PACK DOG

But the sturdier and stronger the dog is, the greater burden he can carry and the more useful he will be on the trail. The alforjas for a dog, or saddle-bags, can be made by anyone who is handy with a needle and thread. A dog pack consists primarily of two bags or pouches (Figs. 209 and 210), with a yoke piece attached to slide over the dog's head and fit across the chest (Figs. 209, 210, 211 and 212). Also a cincha to fasten around the waist or small part of the dog's body, back of its ribs. The pouches (Fig. 210) should have a manta, or cover (Figs. 211, 213, and 214), to keep the rain, snow or dust out of the duffel. Simple bags of strong light material on the pattern of Fig. 210 are best, because the weight of anything unnecessary is to be avoided.

147

THE DOG HITCH

Is not as complicated an affair as the diamond hitch, and anyone who knows how to do up an ordinary parcel can learn the dog hitch by one glance at Figs. 213 and 214.

Slip the breast band over the dog's head, put the saddle-bags well forward on the dog's shoulders, tie the cinch around its waist, after which spread the cover or manta over the bag, and throw the hitch as shown by Figs. 211 and 214. Fig. 213 shows a bundle with a breast band made of the lash rope, in which case the lash rope is usually made of cloth like that in Fig. 211; the whole thing is simplicity itself and a good dog can carry quite a load packed in this manner.

A DOG TRAVOIS

Can also be used at times with advantage, as it was used by our red brothers of the wilderness. Fig. 217 shows a dog harnessed to a travois, made of two shaft poles; the harness consists of a padded collar similar to those used in Northern Quebec for sled dogs, and a cincha of leather or canvas and traces of rope or thong. Figs. 215 and 216 show a rig made by one of my Boy Scouts; the material used was the green saplings cut in the woods, the traces were made of rope manufactured from the roots of the tamarack tree, so also was the cord used to bind the parts of the frame together. The hooks to which the traces were fastened were made of wire nails bent over, and the staples to which the collar was fastened by thongs to the shaft were made of wire nails, the heads of which were ground off by rubbing them on stones; the nails were then bent into the proper curve and driven into the shaft in the form of a staple. Fig. 216 shows the same rig with a leather harness. The American Indian used the

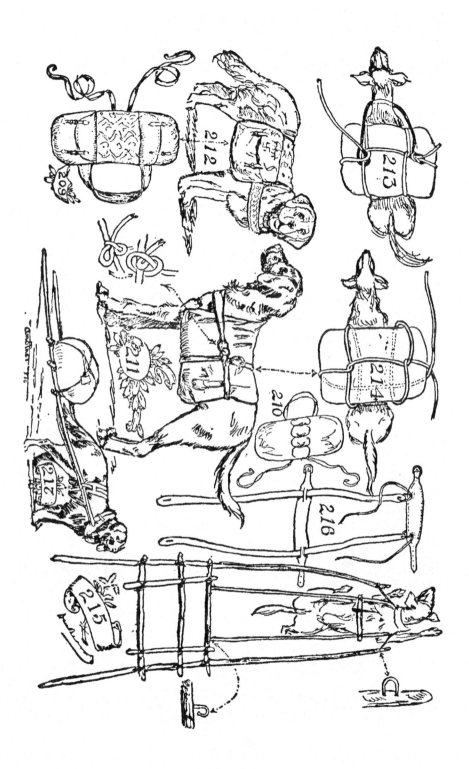

travois on dogs the same as they did upon horses and the sudden appearance of game often produced a stampede of dog travoises, scattering the duffel, including papooses, loaded on the travois.

It is not expected that the reader will make every one of these contrivances, but if he does he will learn How, and to be a good woodsman he *should* know how, so as to be prepared for any emergency. It is possible to make the whole pack for the dog from birch bark, but however it is made, if it serves the purpose of making the dog carry part of the pack, when you put the bark on the dog's back, you will teach the animal that there are two kinds of *barks;* one of which is useful as a duffel bag, and the other as an alarm.

In Alaska and other parts of the far North, as well as in Holland and other parts of Europe, the dog is generally used as a beast of burden; it draws sleds in North America and milk carts and market wagons in Holland, but it is not necessary for us to live in Holland or in the far North in order to make use of the dog; a good dog will cheerfully carry the packs on the trail, loyally guard the camp at night, and, if necessary, die in defense of its master.

Any uncomfortable pack is an abomination; too heavy a pack is an unhappy burden, no pack at all is fine—until you reach camp and hunt around for something to answer for a toothbrush, comb and brush, something on which to sit and sleep, something overhead to protect you from the rains and dews of heaven, something to eat and something to eat with besides your fingers, something from which to drink which holds water better than the hollow of your hand or the brim of your hat, and, in fact, all those necessary little comforts that a fellow wants on an overnight hike. Without these useful articles one will wish that he had subjected himself to the slight fatigue necessary to pack a small pack on his back.

The word "pack" itself is a joy to the outdoor man, for it is only outdoor men who use the word pack for carry, and who call a bundle or load a pack. The reason for this is that the real wilderness man, explorer, prospector, hunter, trapper or scout, packs all his duffel into a bundle which he carries on his back, in two small saddle-bags which are carried by his husky dogs, or a number of well-balanced bundles which are lashed on the pack saddle with a diamond hitch over the back of a pack horse.

You see we have pack dogs, pack horses and pack animals, pack saddles and packers, as well as the packs themselves, which the packers pack and these animals pack on their backs, or which the man himself packs on his own back. Then we also have the pack rat, but the pack rat does not carry things with our consent. The pack rat comes flippity-flop, hopping over the ground from the old hermit, Bill Jones's, packing with him Bill Jones's false teeth which he has abstracted from the tin cup of water at the head of Bill Jones's bunk. The pack rat deposits the teeth at the head of your cot, then deftly picking up your watch, the rat packs it back to Bill Jones's cot and drops it in the tin cup of water, where it soaks until morning.

It is easy to see that however funny the pack rat may be, and however useful he might be to the Sunday comic paper, the rat's humor is not appreciated by the campers in the Rocky Mountains, where it is called a pack rat from its habit of carrying things. Thus it is that in a newly settled country the word "carry" is almost forgotten; one "packs" a letter to the post box, or packs a horse to water, or packs a box of candy to his best girl, or a pail of water from the spring.

MAN PACKING

When you, my good reader, get the pack adjusted on your back and the tump line across your forehead (Fig. 226), remember that you are being initiated into the great fraternity of outdoor people. But no matter how tough or rough you may appear to the casual observer, your roughness is only apparent; a boy or man of refinement carries that refinement inside of him wherever he goes; at the same time when one is carrying a pack on one's back and a tump line on one's forehead (Fig. 226½), or a canoe on one's head, even though a lady should be met on the trail it would not be necessary for one to take off one's hat, for even a foolish society woman would not expect a man to doff the canoe he might be carrying on his head. Under all circumstances use common sense; that is the rule of the wilderness and also of real culture.

The most important thing that you must learn on the trail is not to fret and fume over trifles, and even if your load is heavy and irksome, even though the shoulder straps chafe and the tump line makes your neck ache

DON'T FIGHT YOUR PACK

When we speak of "fighting the pack" we mean fighting the load; that does not mean getting one's load up against a tree and punching it with one's fists or "kicking the stuffings out of it," but it means complaining and fretting because the load is uncomfortable.

There are two kinds of "packs"—the pack that you carry day after day on a long hike, and the pack that you carry when on a canoe trip and you are compelled to leave the water and carry your canoe and duffel overland around some bad rapids or falls. The first-named pack should be as light as possible, say between 30 and 40 pounds, for on a long tramp every pound counts, because *you know that you must carry it* as long as you keep going, and there is no relief in sight except when you stop for your meals or to camp at night. But the last-named pack, the

Portage Pack,

Figs. 218 and 223, the kind that you carry around bad pieces of water, may be as heavy as you can, with safety, load upon your sturdy back, because your mind is buoyed up by the fact that *you know* you will not have to carry that load *very far*, the work will end when you reach the water again, and—strange to say—the mind has as much to do with carrying the load as the muscles. If the mind gives up you will fall helpless even under a small load; if the mind is strong you will stagger along under a very heavy one.

When I asked a friend, who bears the scars of the pack straps on his body, how it was that he managed to endure the torture of such a load, he replied with a grin that as soon as he found that to "fight his pack" meant to perish—meant death!—he made up his mind to forget the blamed thing and so when the pack wearied him and the straps rubbed the skin off his body, he forced himself to think of the good dinners he had had at the Camp-fire Club of America, yum! yum! Also, of all the jolly stories told by the toastmaster, and of the fun he had had at some other entertainments. Often while thinking of these things he caught himself laughing out loud as he trudged along the lone trail, FORGETTING the hateful pack on his back. "In this way," said he, with a winning smile upon his manly and weather-beaten face, "I learned how *not to fight* the pack but to FORGET IT! Then he braced

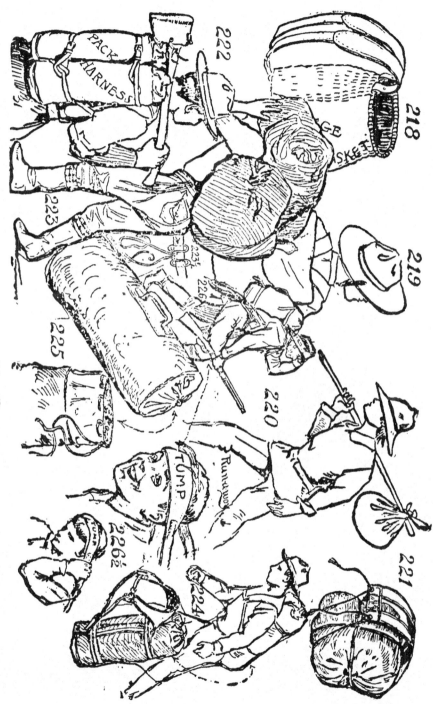

DETAILS OF MAN PACKS

himself up, looked at the snow-capped mountain range ahead, hummed a little cowboy song and trudged on over the frozen snow at a scout's pace.

Now that you know what a pack is, and what "fighting a pack" means, remember that if one's studies at school are hard, that is one's pack. If the work one is doing is hard, difficult or tiresome, that is one's pack. If one's boss is cross and exacting, that is one's pack. If one's parents are worried and forget themselves in their worry and speak sharply, that is one's pack. Don't fight your pack; remember that you are a woodcrafter; straighten your shoulders, put on your scout smile and hit the trail like a man!

If you find that you are tempted to break the Scout Law, that you are tempted at times to forget the Scout Oath, that because your camp mates use language unfit for a wood-crafter or a scout, and you are tempted to do the same, if your playmates play craps and smoke cigarettes, and laugh at you because you refuse to do so, so that you are tempted to join them, these temptations form your pack; don't give in and fall under your load and whimper like a "sissy," or a "mollycoddle," but straighten up, look the world straight in the eye, and hit the trail like a man!

Some of us are carrying portage packs which we can dump off our shoulders at the end of the "carry," some of us are carrying hiking packs which we must carry through life and can never dump from our shoulders until we cross the Grand Portage from which no voyagers ever return. All our packs vary in weight, but none of them is easy to carry if we fret and fume and complain under the load.

We outdoor folks call our load "pack," but our Sunday School teachers sometimes speak of the pack they bear as a "cross." Be it so, but don't fight your pack.

Men Who Have Carried the Pack

The whole north country is sprinkled with the bones of the men who fought their packs. Our own land is also sprinkled with men we call "misfits" and failures, but who are really men who have fought their packs. But every post of eminence in the United States is occupied by a man who forgot his pack; this country was built by men who forgot their packs. George Washington carried a portage pack in weight all through his life, but it was a proud burden and he stood straight under it. Good old Abe Lincoln had even a heavier pack to carry, but in spite of the weight of it he always had a pleasant scout smile for everyone and a merry story to send the visitor away smiling. If Daniel Boone and Simon Kenton had fought their packs we would never have heard of them!

In the illustrations are shown many figures, and one should not forget that these are sketches of real men in the real wilderness, and not fancy pictures drawn from imagination. Figs. 230, 231 and 232 show many different methods of carrying big game on one's shoulders or back. Fig. 232 also shows a couple of prospectors on the trail. One has the bag on his back, held in place by shoulder straps; the other has a bag thrown over his shoulder like a·ragman.

The alpine rucksack will carry—or to speak more properly —with it one can pack a camera, notebook, sketching material, lunch and all those things which a fellow wants on an enjoyable hike. The alpine rucksack is a many-gored poke about 18 inches wide and about 22 inches long without the gores. These pokes can be made so that the gores fold in and produce an ordinary-sized pack, or they may be pushed out like an umbrella so as to make a bag in which one can carry a good-sized boy.

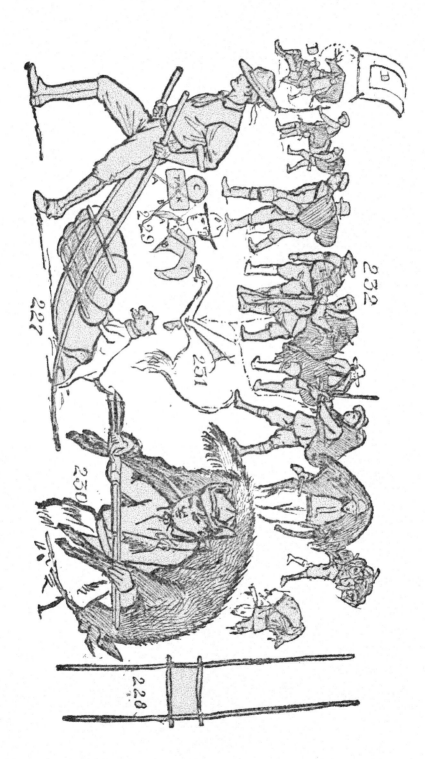

MAN PACKING

THE BROAD BAND

Fig. 232-D shows the broad band used by the men of the far north. The reader will note that the broad canvas bands come over the shoulders from the top of the pack; also that a broad breast band connects the shoulder bands, while rope, whang strings or thongs run through eyelets in the band and to the bottom of the pack. This is said to be the most comfortable pack used and has an interesting history; it was evolved from an old pair of overalls. There was a Hebrew peddler who followed the gold seekers and he took a pair of canvas overalls and put them across his breast, and to the legs he fastened the pack upon his back. The overalls being wide and broad did not cut his chest, as do smaller straps, thongs or whang strings.

But breast straps of any kind are not now recommended by all authorities. It is claimed that they interfere with the breathing and a fellow "mouching" along the trail needs to have his chest free to expand, for not only his speed but his endurance depends upon the free action of his lungs.

THE TUMP

Figs. 226 and 226½ show the use of the celebrated tump strap. This tump strap is used from Central America to the Arctic Circle. The Mexican water carrier uses it to tote his burden; the Tete Bule Indian and the Montenais Indian in the Northeast also carry their packs with a tump line.

Fig. 226½ shows how the tump line is made. It is a strap or lash rope with a broad band to fit over the packer's head, and thus relieve the weight which the shoulders have to bear.

Fig. 218 shows the well-known portage pack basket which is used by the guides in the Adirondack regions. Fig. 219 shows the Nessmuk knapsack. Fig. 222 shows a pack harness

11

of straps by which two duffel bags are borne on the back. Fig. 225 shows a duffel bag which is laced up at one end with a thong; also the end of the bag open.

The Duffel Bag is Useful

The duffel bag is the ideal poke in which to pack one's belongings. It is waterproof, it makes a good pillow, a far better pillow than an axe and pair of boots on which I myself have rested my weary head many a night, and it also makes a good cushion upon which to sit. The duffel bag may be procured from any outfitting establishment. The ones I own are now shiny with dirt and grease, gathered from the camps and forests extending from Maine to the State of Washington, from Northern Quebec to Florida. I love the old bags, for even though they be greasy and shiny, and blackened with the charcoals of many campfires, they are chuck full of delightful memories.

Fig. 220 is the old-time poke made of a bandanna handkerchief, with its ends tied together and swung over a stick.

This is the pack, a cut of which may be found in all the old newspapers antedating the Civil War, where runaway negroes are advertised. It is the sort of pack respectable tramps used to carry, back in the times when tramps were respectable. It is the kind of pack I find represented in an old oil painting hanging on my dining-room wall, which was painted by some European artist back in the seventeenth century. When fellows carry the runaway pack they are "traveling light."

Fig. 229 shows how to construct a makeshift pack. A rope of cedar bark is arranged with a loop C (Fig. 229), for the yoke the ends A and B are brought up under the arms and tied to the yoke C, which then makes a breast band.

For a long hike thirty pounds is enough for a big boy to carry, and it will weigh three hundred and fifty pounds at the end of a hard day's tramp. Heavy packs, big packs, like those shown in Fig. 223, are only used on a portage, that is, for short distance. Of course, you fellows know that in all canoe trips of any consequence one must cross overland from one lake to another, or overland above a waterfall to a safe place below it, or around quick water, or to put it in the words of tenderfeet, water which is too quick for canoe travel, around tumultuous rapids where one must carry his canoe and duffel. But these carries or portages are seldom long. The longest I remember of making was a trifle over five miles in length.

Remember that the weight of a load depends a great deal upon your mind. Consequently for a long distance the load should be light; for a short distance the only limit to the load is the limit of the packer's strength.

But

People differ so in regard to how to carry a pack and what kind of a pack to carry, that the author hesitates to recommend any particular sort; personally he thinks that a pack harness hitched on to the duffel bags (Figs. 221, 222 and 224), is the proper and practical thing. Duffel bags, by the way, are water-proof canvas bags (Fig. 225), made of different sizes, in which to pack one's clothes, food, or what not. The portage basket (Fig. 218), is a favorite in the Adirondacks, but it is not a favorite with the writer; the basket itself is heavy and to his mind unnecessary, the knapsack (Fig. 219), is good for short hikes when one does not have to carry much. The best way for the reader to do is to experiment, see how much of a load he can carry; fifty pounds is more than enough for a big strong man to carry all day long, day in and day out, and forty pounds is more than he wants to carry, but a good husky boy may be able to carry forty pounds on his back. At the Army and Navy stores and at the outfitter's you can find all sorts of duffel bags and knapsacks, and at any of the big outfitting stores they will tell you just what kind of baggage you will need for the particular trip, for some-one in the stores has been over the very ground that you are going over, for all the clerks and proprietors of the out-fitting stores are sportsmen. But—yes, there is a "but"—the real genuine American boy will construct his own outfit duffel bags, mess kit and tents.

CHAPTER IX

PREPARING FOR CAMPING TRIP

CHAPTER IX

PREPARING FOR CAMPING TRIP

MANY people are so accustomed to have other people wait upon them that they are absolutely funny when you meet them in the woods; when their canoe runs its prow up upon the sandy beach and there is a portage to make, such people stand helplessly around waiting for some red-capped porter to come and take their baggage, but the only red caps in the woods are the red-headed woodpeckers and they will see you in Germany before they will help tote your duffel across the portage.

When one gets into the real woods, even if it is only in Maine, Wisconsin, the Adirondacks, or the Southern pine forests, one soon discovers that there are no drug stores around the corner, the doctor is a long way off, the butcher, the baker, the candle-stick maker, trolley cars, telephone and taxi cabs are not within reach, sight or hearing; then a fellow begins to realize that it is "up to" himself to tote his own luggage, to build his own fires, to make his own shelters, and even to help put up the other fellows' tents, or to cook the meals. Yes, and to wash the dishes, too!

One reason we outdoor people love the woods is that it develops self-reliance and increases our self-respect by increasing our ability to do things; we love the work, we love the hardship, we like to get out of sight of the becapped maids, the butler and the smirking waiters waiting for a tip, and for the same reason the real honest-to-goodness American boys love a camp. Why bless your soul!—every one of them in his inmost heart regrets that he did not live away back in the time when the long-haired Wetzel, Daniel Boone and

Simon Kenton roved the woods, or at least back when Colonel Bill Cody, Buffalo Jones and Yellowstone Kelly were dashing over the plains with General Miles, General Bell and the picturesque blond, long-haired General Custer.

Sometimes the author is himself guilty of such wishes, and he used to dream of those days when he was a barefooted boy. But, honest now, is it not really too bad that there are no longer any hostile Indians? And what a pity that improved firearms have made the big game so very shy that it is afraid of a man with a gun!

But cheer up, the joy of camping is not altogether ruined, because we do not have to fight all day to save our scalps from being exported, or even because the grizzly bears refuse to chase us up a tree, and the mountain lions or "painters" decline to drop from an overhanging limb on our backs.

Remember that all things come to him who will but wait: that is, if he works for these things while he is doing the waiting. The Chief has spent his time and energy for the last thirty odd years hammering away at two ideas: the big outdoors for the boys, and Americanism for all the people. Thank the Lord, he has lived long enough to see the boys stampede for the open and the people for Americanism.

Because of the stampede for the open, in which people of all ages have joined, there are so many kinds of camps nowadays: scout camps, soldier camps, training camps, recreation camps, girls' camps and boys' camps, that it is somewhat difficult for a writer to tell what to do in order to "Be Prepared." There are freight car side-track camps, gypsy wagon camps, houseboat camps, old-fashioned camp-meeting camps and picnic camps; the latter dot the shores of New Jersey, the lake sides at Seattle, and their tents are mingled with big black boulders around Spokane; you will find them on the shores of Devil's Lake, North Dakota, and in the few groves that are back of Winnipeg, Manitoba.

But such camps have little attraction for the real hard-boiled camper, and have no better claim to being the real thing than the more or less grand palaces built in the woods, camouflaged outside with logs or bark, and called "camps" by their untruthful owners; such people belittle the name of camp and if they want to be honest they should stick to the bungling bungalow—but wait a minute—even that is far-fetched; the bungalow belongs in East India and looks as much like one of these American houses as a corn-crib does like a church.

When we talk of camping we mean living under bark, brush or canvas in the "howling wilderness," or as near a howling wilderness as our money and time will permit us to reach; in other words, we want a camp in the wildest place we can find, except when we go to our own scout camp, and even then we like it better if it is located in a wild, romantic spot.

How to Get Ready for Camp

There are some little personal things to which one should give one's attention before starting on a long trip. If it is going to be a real wild camping trip it is best to go to the barber shop and get a good hair cut just before one starts. Also one should trim one's nails down as close as comfort will allow. Long nails, if they are well manicured, will do for the drawing room and for the office, but in camp they have a habit of turning back (Fig. 232)—and gee willikens, how they hurt! Or they will split down into the quick (Fig. 233) and that hurts some, too! So trim them down snug and close; do it before you start packing up your things, or you may hurt your fingers while packing. But even before trimming your nails

Go to Your Dentist

And insist upon him making an examination of every tooth in your head; a toothache is bad enough anywhere, goodness knows, but a toothache away out in the woods with no help in sight will provoke a saint to use expressions not allowed by the Scout Manual. The Chief knows what he is talking about—he has been there! He once rode over Horse Plains alongside of a friend who had a bad tooth, and the friend was a real saint! His jaw was swelled out like a rubber balloon, but he did not use one naughty word on the trip, notwithstanding every jolt of that horse was like sticking a knife in him.

The writer could not help it; he was thoughtlessly cruel and he laughed at his friend's lugubrious expression—Take heed, do not be as cruel as was the writer, for sooner or later you will pay for such thoughtless levity. It was only next season, away up in the mountains of the British possessions on the Pacific Coast, that the friend's turn came to laugh at the author as the latter nursed an ulcerated tooth. Wow! Wow! Wow!

Well, never mind the details, they are too painful to talk about, but remember the lesson that they teach—Go to the Dentist and get a clean bill of health on the tooth question before you start for a lengthy camp.

A Buckskin Man's Pocket

When we speak of his pocket that includes all of his clothes, because on the inside of his coat, if he wears one, are stuck an array of safety pins (Fig. 234), but usually the pins are fastened onto his shirt. A safety pin is as useful to a man in camp as is a hairpin to a woman, and a woman can camp with no other outfit but a box of hairpins. One can

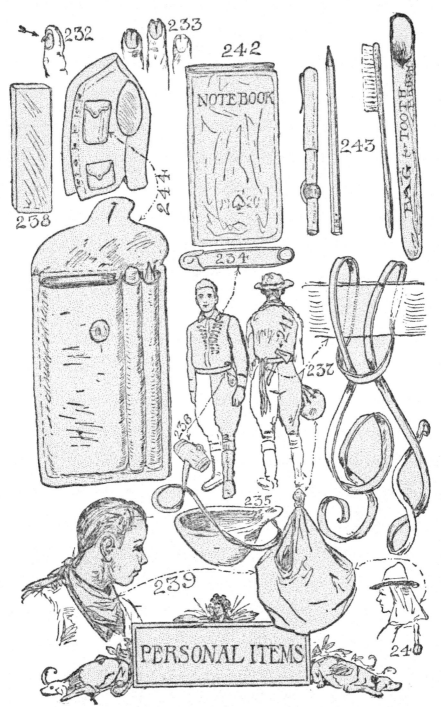

A Buckskin's Pocket

use safety pins for clothespins when one's socks are drying at night, one can use them to pin up the blankets and thus make a sleeping-bag of them, or one can use them for the purpose of temporarily mending rips and tears in one's clothes. These are only a few of the uses of the safety pin on the trail. After one has traveled with safety pins one comes to believe that they are almost indispensable.

In one of the pockets there should be a lot of bachelor buttons, the sort that you do not have to sew on to your clothes, but which fasten with a snap, something like glove buttons. There should be a pocket made in your shirt or vest to fit your notebook (Fig. 244), and a part of it stitched up to hold a pencil and a toothbrush. Your mother can do this at home for you before you leave. Then you should have a good jack-knife; I always carry my jack-knife in my hip pocket. A pocket compass, one that you have tested before starting on your trip, should lodge comfortably in one of your pockets, and hitched in your belt should be your noggin carved from a burl from a tree (Fig. 235); it should be carried by slipping the toggle (Fig. 236) underneath the belt. Also in the belt you should carry some whang strings (Fig. 237); double the whang strings up so that the two ends come together, tuck the loop through your belt until it comes out at the other side, then put the two ends of the string through the loop and the whang strings are fast but easily pulled out when needed; whang strings are the same as belt lashings. A small whetstone (Fig. 238) can find a place somewhere about your clothes, probably in the other hip pocket, and it is most useful, not only with which to put an edge on your knife but also on your axe.

Inside the sweat band of your hat, or around the crown on the outside of your hat, carry a gut leader with medium-

sized artificial flies attached, and around your neck knot a
big gaudy bandanna handkerchief (Fig. 239); it is a most useful article; it can be used in which to carry your game, food
or duffel, or for warmth, or worn over the head for protection
from insects (Fig. 240). In the latter case put it on your
head under your hat and allow it to hang over your shoulders
like the havelock worn by the soldiers of '61·

Carry your belt axe thrust through your belt at your back
(Fig. 241), where it will be out of the way, not at your side
as you do on parade.

No camper, be he hunter, fisherman, scout, naturalist,
explorer, prospector, soldier or lumberman, should go into
the woods without a notebook and hard lead pencil (Fig. 242).
Remember that notes made with a hard pencil will last longer
than those made with ink, and be readable as long as the
paper lasts.

Every scientist and every surveyor knows this and it
is only tenderfeet, who use a soft pencil and fountain pen
for making field notes, because an upset canoe will blur all
ink marks and the constant rubbing of the pages of the book
will smudge all soft pencil marks.

Therefore, have a pocket especially made (Fig. 244), so
that your notebook, pencil and fountain pen (Fig. 243), if
you insist upon including it—will fit snugly with no chance
of dropping out; also make a separate pocket for your toothbrush which should be kept in an oil-skin bag (Fig. 243).

A piece of candle (Fig. 245) is not only a most convenient
thing with which to light a fire on a rainy day, but it has
ofttimes proved a life saver to Northern explorers benumbed
with the cold.

It is a comparatively easy thing to light a candle under
the shelter of one's hat or coat, even in a driving rain. When

one's fingers are numb or even frosted, and with the candle flame one can start a life-saving fire; so do not forget your candle stub as a part of your pocket outfit.

In the black fly belt it is wise to add a bottle of fly dope (Fig. 251) to one's personal equipment. If you make your own fly dope have a slow fire and allow to simmer over it

3 oz. pine tar
2 oz. castor oil
1 oz. pennyroyal

or heat 3 oz. of pine tar with two oz. of olive oil and then stir in 1 oz. of pennyroyal, 1 oz. of citronella, 1 oz. of creosote and 1 oz. of camphor.

If you propose traveling where there are black flies and mosquitoes, let your mother sew onto a pair of old kid gloves some chintz or calico sleeves that will reach from your wrists to above your elbow (Fig. 246), cut the tips of the fingers off the gloves so that you may be able to use your hands handily, and have an elastic in the top of the sleeve to hold them onto your arm. Rigged thus, the black flies and mosquitoes can only bite the ends of your fingers, and, sad to say, they will soon find where the ends of the fingers are located.

A piece of cheese cloth, fitted over the hat to hang down over the face, will protect that part of your anatomy from insects (Fig. 246), but if they are not very bad use fly dope (Fig. 251), and add a bottle of it to your pocket outfit. One doesn't look pretty when daubed up with fly dope, but we are in the woods for sport and adventure and not to look pretty. Our vanity case has no lip stick, rouge or face powder; it only possesses a toothbrush and a bottle of fly dope.

Certain times of year, when one goes camping in the neighborhood of the trout brooks, one needs to BE PREPARED, for one can catch more trout and enjoy fishing better if protected against the attacks of the black flies, mosquitoes, midges and "no-see-ums."

Anything swung by a strap across one's shoulder will in time "cut" the shoulders painfully unless they are protected by a pad (Fig. 246½). A few yards of mosquito netting or cheese cloth occupies little space and is of little weight, but

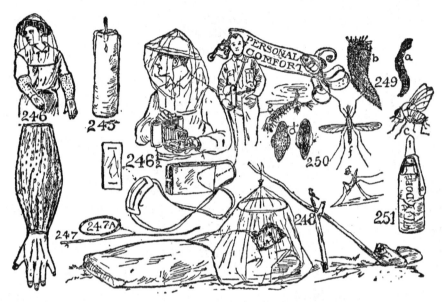

is very useful as a protection at night. Bend a wand (Fig. 247) into a hoop and bind the ends together (Fig. 247A), with safety pins; pin this in the netting and suspend the net from its center by a stick (Fig. 248).

The black fly, C (Fig. 249), is a very small hump-backed pest, the young (larvæ) (Fig. 249a) live in cold, clear running water; Fig. 249b is the cocoon.

There are many kinds of mosquitoes; all of them are Bolsheviks, and with the black flies and other vermin they argue that since nature made them with blood suckers and provided you with the sort of blood that they like, they have an inherent right to suck your blood—and they do it!

But some mosquitoes are regular Huns and professional germ carriers, and besides annoying one they skillfully insert the germs of malaria and yellow fever into one's system. The malaria mosquitoes are known as anopheles. The highbrow name for the United States malaria distributor is "Anopheles quadrimaculatus" (Fig. 250 F). It is only the females that you need fear; drone bees do not sting and buck mosquitoes do not bite.

Fig. 250d shows lower and upper side of the anopheles's egg. Fig. 250e is the wiggler or larvæ of the anopheles; the anopheles likes to let the blood run to its head, and any careful observer will know him at a glance from his pose while resting (Fig. 250g).

Of course, you will not need fly dope on the picnic grounds, and you will not need your pocket compass on the turnpike hike, and you will not need your jack-knife with which to eat at the boarding house or hotel, but we Boy Scouts are the real thing; we go to hotels and boarding houses and picnics when we must, but not when we can find real adventure in wilder places. We shout:

There is life in the roar of plunging streams,
There is joy in the campfire's blaze at night.
Hark! the elk bugles, the panther screams!
And the shaggy bison roll and fight.
Let your throbbing heart surge and bound,
List to the whoop of the painted Reds;
Pass the flapjacks merrily round
As the gray wolf howls in the river beds.

We weary of our cushions of rest;
God of our Fathers, give back our West.
What care we for luxury and ease?
Darn the tall houses, give us tall trees!

However crude these verses may be, the sentiment is all right. But may be it will express our idea better if we do not attempt rhyme. Suppose we try it this way—

Listen to the whistle of the marmots;
The hooting of the barred owl, the bugling of the elk!
The yap, yap, yap of the coyote, the wild laugh of the loon;
The dismal howl of the timber wolf,
The grunting of the bull moose, the roaring of the torrent,
And the crashing thunder of the avalanche!

Ah, that's the talk; these are the words and sounds that make the blood in one's veins tingle like ginger ale. Why do all red-blooded men and real American boys like to hear

The crunching of the dry snow;
The flap, flap, flap of snowshoes;
The clinking of the spurs and bits;
The creaking of the saddle leather;
The breathing of the bronco;
The babbling of the rivulet;
The whisper of the pines,
The twitter of the birds,
And the droning of bees.

Why? Because in these sounds we get the dampness of the moss, the almond-like odor of twin flowers, the burning dryness of the sand, the sting of the frost, the grit of the rocks and the tang of old mother earth! They possess the magic power of suggestion. By simply repeating these words we transport our souls to the wilderness, set our spirits free, and we are once again what God made us; natural and normal boys, listening to nature's great runes, odes, epics, lyrics, poems, ballads and roundelays, as sung by God's own bards!

PACKING

When packing, remember that a partly filled bag (Fig. 252) is easy to pack, easy to carry on one's shoulders; but a tightly filled bag (Fig. 253) is a nuisance on the trail. When

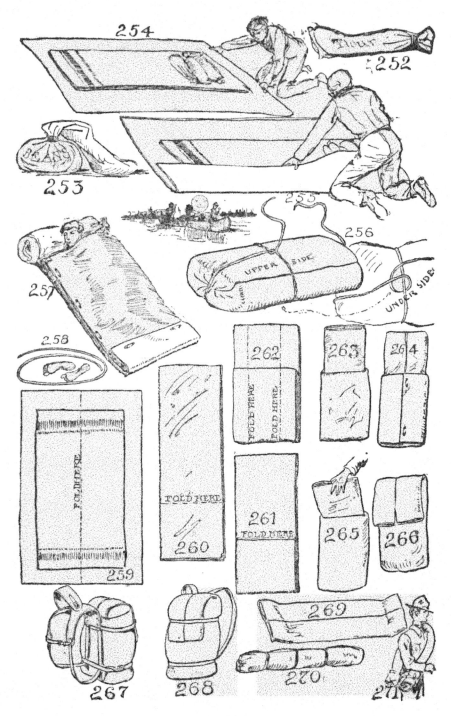

MAKING A PACK

Making a Pack

To ship as baggage, fold the blankets lengthwise (Fig. 254), place them in the middle of your tarpaulin or floor cloth (Fig. 254); fold the cover over (Fig. 255), then tuck in the ends and roll the package into a bundle and cinch (Figs. 255 and 256). A

Sleeping-Bag

Can be improvised from one's blankets by the use of safety pins (Fig. 257). A section of the bag (Fig. 258) shows how the blankets are doubled. To make a

Back Pack

Fold as in Fig. 259, then bend up the end as indicated by Figs. 260 and 261, fold again, Fig. 262, then fold in the two edges, Figs. 263 and 264, which show both sides of pack; bend over the top, Figs. 265 and 266, and strap ready to carry, Figs. 267 and 268. For a

Blanket Roll

Fold as in Fig. 269; bend in the ends and roll (Fig. 270). Strap or lash the ends together (Fig. 271).

CHAPTER X

SADDLES

HOW TO CHOOSE A SADDLE

EVOLUTION OF THE MEXICAN SADDLE

BIRTH OF THE BLUFF FRONTED SADDLE

THE COWBOY AGE

SAWBUCKS OR PACK SADDLES

STRAIGHT LEG AND BENT KNEE

NAMES OF PARTS OF SADDLE

CENTER FIRE AND DOUBLE CINCH

CHAPTER X

SADDLES

WE know that comparatively few of our boys take their hikes on horseback, especially their camping hikes. But a lot of their daddies and big brothers do take their horse, and the pack horse on their hunting and fishing trips, and every boy wants to know how to do the things his daddy knows how to do. Besides all that, the author is aware of the fact that the daddies and the uncles and the big brothers are reading all the stuff he puts out for the boys. They are constantly quoting to the author things that he has said to the boys, so that now in writing a book for the boys he must count them in.

CHOOSE A SADDLE THAT FITS

Everyone knows the misery of an ill-fitting shoe, and no one in his right mind would think of taking a prolonged hike in shoes that pinched his feet, but everybody does not know that a saddle should fit the rider; an ill-fitting saddle can cause almost as much discomfort as an ill-fitting shoe. The best all-around sportsman's saddle in the world is the cowboy saddle of the West. A writer in the *Saturday Evening Post*, who has written a delightfully intelligent article on saddles, in speaking of the Western cow-puncher's saddle, says:

"There are many good riders who have never thrown a leg over any other sort of saddle, and for work on the plains or in the mountains no man who has used one would ever care for any other type. It is as much a distinct product of this continent as is the birch bark canoe or the American axe or rifle."

185

Like the cowboy hat, the diamond hitch and the lariat, the cowboy saddle is evolved from the Spanish adaptation of the Moorish saddle. The old-fashioned Spanish saddle with the heavy wooden block stirrups, not the bent wood stirrups, but the big stirrups made out of blocks of wood (Fig. 273);such a saddle with stirrups often weighed over sixty pounds. These saddles were garnished with silver and gold, and the spurs that the rancheros wore had big wheels with "bells" on them, and spikes long enough to goad the thick skin of an elephant. I formerly possessed one of the picturesque old saddles on which all the leather work was engraved by hand, by the use of some tool like a graver, probably a sharpened nail; consequently none of the designs was duplicated.

In the good old cow days there were two sorts of saddles: the "California Center Fire" and the "Texas Double Chinch," and all those that I remember seeing had rather a short horn at the bow with a very broad top sometimes covered with a silver plate; the seat was also much longer than it is to-day.

Fig. 272 shows a military saddle which is a modified cowboy saddle, and Fig. 274 shows a comparatively modern cowboy saddle. The up-to-date saddle of to-day has a bulge in front, not shown on the diagram.

In the olden days there were no societies for the prevention of cruelty to animals, and on the ranges horses were plenty; therefore, when one of the long-haired plainsmen, with his long rifle in front of him on the long saddle, and the heavy Spanish-American trappings to the horse, killed the horse by overwork, he simply took off his saddle and trappings, caught another horse, mounted it and continued his journey; there were plenty of horses—why should he worry?

Later when the cowboy age came in, the cowboys themselves on the Southern ranges used the Spanish-American

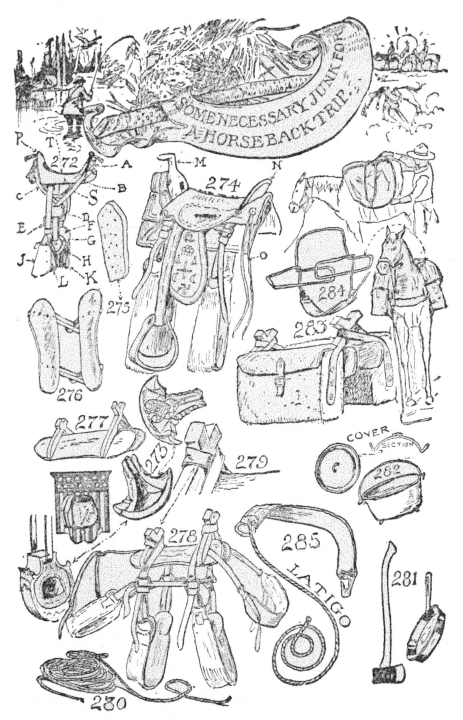

PACK TRAIN OUTFIT

outfit; the only blessing the poor horse had was the blanket under the saddle.

When the block wooden stirrups were abandoned and the thinner oval stirrups adopted, the latter were protected by long caps of leather, the dangling ends of which were silver tipped. The cowboys themselves wore heavy leather breeches called chaps (an abbreviation of the Spanish chaparejo). Thus with the feet and legs protected they could ride through the cactus plants and dash through the mesquite country without fear of being pricked by the thorns, no matter what happened to the horse. Not only did this leather armor protect them from thorns and branches, but it also prevented many a broken leg resulting from kicks by burros, mules and horses.

The rolled coat or blanket, which the bronco busters on the lower ranges in early times lashed across the horse in front of their seat, is the thing from which the bucking roll was evolved, and the buckskin bucking roll, we are told, is the daddy of the swell or bulged front saddle now used.

The old-fashioned cowboy saddle has a narrow front, but about two decades ago

THE VIDALIA SADDLE-TREE

Migrated slowly from California over the plains, and was the first one to show the bulged front, and to change the narrow bow of the cow saddle to the bluff bow of the saddle as used to-day. It is claimed that while this protects the rider from injuries more or less, it has a tendency not to give a fellow the opportunity of as firm a grip with his legs as did the old narrow bowed cowboy seat. Later, in Oregon, they began to manufacture "incurved saddles," so that the rider's legs could fit better under the front, and the Wyoming saddle makers caught the idea, so that to-day the vanishing race of cowboys are using saddles, which it would have taken a brave man to straddle in the early days, not because the saddle is dangerous but because it would have looked funny to the old-time boys, and they would not have been slow in giving expression to boisterous and discomforting merriment.

It is an odd thing, this law of growth or evolution, and it *is a law*, and a fixed law, certain peculiarities go together; for instance, if one goes systematically to work to produce fan-tail pigeons, one finds that he is also producing pigeons with feathered legs. The breeders have also discovered that in producing a chicken with silky white feathers they unwillingly produce a fowl with black meat. What has this got to do with saddles? Only that the same law holds good here: the more the front bulges in the saddle the more the horns shrivel, developing a tendency to rake forward and upward; the stirrups also dwindle in size. The saddle, which the writer possessed, has stirrups made of iron rings covered with leather and the caps were lined with sheep's wool. We read that now the narrow half-round oval stirrup is a favorite with the cow-punchers, which the cowboy uses with his foot thrust all the way in so that the weight of the rider rests upon the middle of the foot. This is as disturbing to the European idea of "proper form" as was the Declaration of Independence, but the Declaration of Independence has proved its efficiency by its results; so also has it been proved that for those who ride all day long the nearer they can come to standing on their feet, and at the same time relieving the feet of the total weight of the body by resting it on the saddle, the easier it is to stay in the saddle for long stretches of time; in other words, the more comfortable the saddle, the longer one can occupy it without discomfort, and that is the reason a saddle should fit the rider.

With Western Horses

One must use Western ways; remember the horses were educated in the West if you were not, but it is not necessary to use the cruel, old jaw-breaking Spanish bits with a ring on them. I have one, but it only hangs on the studio wall as a souvenir and a curious object of torture. But don't try a straight bit on a Western horse; he may spit it out and laugh at you; use the modern Western bits, saddles, and cinch and you will not go far wrong. Of course

The Pack Horse

Is another proposition, for here you will need a pack sawbuck saddle (Figs. 276, 277, 278 and 279); over this saddle you can swing your two saddle bags, called alforjas (Fig. 283). Fig. 284 is after Stewart Edward White's diagram, and shows how the alforjas are lashed fast to the horse's back with a latigo (Fig. 285). Fig. 280 is the lash rope which the man above Fig. 284 is using. In Chapter VII we tell how to throw the diamond hitch. Fig. 282 shows the cowboy favorite cooking utensil, the old Dutch oven, and it is practically the same model as the one once belonging to Abraham Lincoln. A glance at the cross-section of the cover shows you how the edges are dented in to hold the hot ashes heaped on top of it when the bake oven is being used. Fig. 281 is a sketch of two essentials for any sort of a trip: an axe and a frying pan.

Of course, one could write a whole book on horseback work, saddles and pack saddles. The truth is that one could write a whole book on any subject or any chapter in this book. But my aim is to start you off right; I believe that the way to learn to do a thing Is To Do It, and not depend upon your book knowledge. Therefore, when I write a book for you boys, I do the best I know how to make you understand

what I am talking about, and to excite in your mind and heart
a desire to do the things talked of; you must remember, however, that no one ever could learn to skate from a school of
correspondence or a book, but one could gain a great deal
of useful knowledge about anything from a useful book,
knowledge that will be of great help when one is trying to do
the things treated of in the book.

I can tell you with the aid of diagrams how to pack a
blanket, and you can follow my diagrams and pack your
blanket; but in order to ride, skate, swim or dance, you must
gain the skill by practice. A book, however, can tell you the
names of the part of the things.

Names of Parts of Saddle

For instance (Fig. 272), T is the saddle-tree; a good
saddle-tree is made of five stout pieces of cottonwood which
are covered with rawhide; when the rawhide shrinks it draws
the pieces together more tightly and perfectly than they could
be fastened by tongue and groove, glue, screws or nails; in
fact, it makes one solid piece of the whole. The horn is
fastened on to the tree by its branched legs, and covered with
leather or braided rawhide. The shanks are covered first and
then attached to the tree and the thongs are tacked to the
saddle-tree, after which the bulged cover is fitted on. When
a good saddle-tree is finished it is as much one piece as is
the pelvis of a skeleton.

P is the pummel, A is the cantle, S is the side bar of the
saddle-tree, C is a quarter strap side, B is the quarter strap
cantle, E is the stirrup buckle, F is the outer strap safe, G is
the cincha ring, H is the cincha cover; the cincha strap is
unlettered but it connects the cincha ring with the quarter
strap ring D; J is the cap or leather stirrup cover, L is the

wooden stirrup, K is the horsehair cincha. Fig. 275 is one of the saddle pads to fit under the saddle. On Fig. 274M is the horn, N the cantle, O the whang leather, which your saddler will call tie strings.

You will note that in Fig. 274 there are two cinchas, and in Fig. 272 but one. You will also note that in Fig. 274 the skirt of your saddle seems to be double, or even triple, and the stirrup rigging comes on top of the skirt, and this is made up of the back jockey, front jockey, and side jockey or seat. Now then, you know all about horseback; there is nothing more I can tell you about the pack horse, but remember not to swell up with pride because of your vast knowledge, and try to ride an outlaw horse with an Eastern riding school bit. But acknowledge yourself a tenderfoot, a short horn, a shavetail, a Cheechako, and ask your Western friends to let you have a horse that knows all the tricks of his trade, but who has a compassionate heart for a greenhorn. There are lots of such good fellows among the Western horses, and they will treat you kindly. I know it because I have tried them, and as I said before, I make no boast of being a horse-man myself. When I get astride of a Western horse I lean over and whisper in his ear, and confess to him just how green I am, and then put him on his honor to treat me white, and so far he has always done so.

CHAPTER XI

CHOOSING A CAMP SITE

CHAPTER XI

CHOOSING A CAMP SITE

WHEN choosing a camp site, if possible, choose a forest or grove of young trees. First, because of the shade they give you; secondly, because they protect you from storms, and thirdly, because they protect you from lightning.

Single trees, or small groups of trees in open pastures are exceedingly dangerous during a thunder storm; tall trees on the shores of a river or lake are particularly selected as targets for thunder bolts by the storm king. But the safest place in a thunder storm, next to a house, is a forest. The reason of this is that each wet tree is a lightning rod silently conducting the electric fluid without causing explosions. Do not camp at the foot of a very tall tree, or an old tree with dead branches on it, for a high wind may break off the branches and drop them on your head with disastrous results; the big tree itself may fall even when there is no wind at all.

Once I pitched my camp near an immense tree on the Flathead Indian Reservation. A few days later we returned to our old camp. As we stopped and looked at the site where our tents had been pitched we looked at each other solemnly, but said nothing, for there, prone upon the ground, lay that giant veteran tree!

But young trees do not fall down, and if they did they could not create the havoc caused by the immense bole of the patriarch of the forest when it comes crashing to the earth. A good scout must "Be Prepared," and to do so must remember that safety comes first, and too close neighborhood to a big tree is often unsafe.

Remember to choose the best camp site that can be found; do not travel all day, and as night comes on stop at any old place; but in the afternoon keep your eyes open for likely spots.

Halt early enough to give time to have everything snug and in order before dark.

In selecting camping ground, look for a place where good water and wood are handy. Choose a high spot with a gentle slope if possible; guard your spring or water hole from animals, for if the day is hot your dog will run ahead of the party and jump into the middle of the spring to cool himself, and horses and cattle will befoul the water.

If camping in the Western states on the shores of a shallow stream which lies along the trail, cross the stream before making camp or you may not be able to cross it for days. A chinook wind suddenly melting the snows in the distant mountains, or a cloud-burst miles and miles up stream, may suddenly send down to you a dangerous flood even in the dry season. I have known of parties being detained for days by one of these sudden roaring floods of water, which came unannounced, the great bole of mud, sticks and logs sweeping by their camp and taking with it everything in its path.

A belt of dense timber between camp and a pond or swamp will act as a protection from mosquitoes. As a rule, keep to windward of mosquito holes; the little insects travel with the wind, not against it. 'Ware ant hills, rotten wood infested with ants, for they make poor bedfellows and are a nuisance where the food is kept.

A bare spot on the earth, where there are no dry leaves, is a wind-swept spot; where the dust-covered leaves lie in heaps the wind does not blow. A windy place is generally free from mosquitoes, but it is a poor place to build a fire;

a small bank is a great protection from high wind and twisters. During one tornado I had a camp under the lee of a small elevation; we only lost the fly of one tent out of a camp of fifty or more, while in more exposed places nearby great trees were uprooted and houses unroofed.

It must not be supposed that the camping season is past because the summer vacation is over. The real camping season begins in the Wild Rice Moon, that is, September. Even if school or business takes all our time during the week, we still have week-ends in which to camp. Saturday has always been a boys' day. Camping is an American institution, because America affords the greatest camping ground in the world.

The author is seated in his own log house, built by himself, on the shores of Big Tink Pond. Back of him there is pitched a camp of six rows of tents, which are filled with a joyful, noisy crowd of youngsters.

It is here in the mountains of Pike County, Pennsylvania, where the bluestone is stratified in horizontal layers, that one may study the camp from its very birth to the latest and finished product of this century.

Everywhere in these mountains there are outcroppings of the bluestone, and wherever the face of a ridge of this stone is exposed to the elements, the rains or melting snows cause the water to drip from the earth on top of the stone and trickle down over the face of the cliff. Then, when a cold snap turns the moisture into ice in every little crack in the rock, the expansion of the ice forces the sides of the cracks apart at the seams in the rock until loose pieces from the undersides slide off, leaving small spaces over which the rock projects. The little caves thus made make retreats for white-footed mice and other small mammals, chipmunks and cave rats. When these become deeper they may become dens in which snakes sleep through the winter.

The openings never grow smaller, and in course of time are large enough for the coon, then the fox, and in olden times they made dens for wolves and panthers, or a place where the bear would "hole" up for the winter.

Time is not considered by Dame Nature; she has no trains to catch, and as years and centuries roll by the little openings in the bluestone become big enough to form a shelter for a crouching man, and the crouching man used them as a place in which to camp when the Norsemen in their dragon ships were braving the unknown ocean. When Columbus, with his toy boats, was blundering around the West Indies, the crouching man was camping under the bluestone ledges of old Pike County, Pennsylvania. There he built his camp-fires and cooked his beaver and bear and deer and elk, using dishes of pottery of his own make and ornamented with crude designs traced in the clay before the dishes were baked.

We know all this to be true history, because within a short walk of the author's log house there are overhanging ledges of bluestone, and underneath these ledges we, ourselves, have crouched and camped, and with sharp sticks have dug up the ground from the layer of earth covering the floor rock. And in this ground we have found bits of pottery, the split bones of different wild animals—split so that the savage camper might secure the rich marrow from the inside of the bones—arrowheads, bone awls and needles, tomahawks, the skulls of beaver and spearheads; all these things have been found under the overhanging bluestone.

Wherever such a bluestone ledge exists, one may make a good camp by closing up the front of the cave with sticks against the overhanging cliff and thatching the sticks with browse or balsam boughs, thus making the simplest form of a lean-to. The Indians used such shelters before the advent of the white man; Daniel Boone used them when he first visited Kentucky and, in spite of the great improvement in tents, the overhanging ledge is still used in Pennsylvania by fishermen and hunters for overnight camps.

But if one uses such a site for his overnight camp or his week's-end camp, one should not desecrate the ancient abode by introducing under its venerable roof, modern up-to-date cooking and camp material, but should exercise ingenuity and manufacture, as far as possible, the conveniences and furniture necessary for the camp.

Since the author is writing this in a camp in the woods, he will tell the practical things that confront him, even though he must mention a white man's shop broom.

In the first place, the most noticeable defect in the tenderfoot's work is the manner in which he handles his broom and wears the broom out of shape. A broom may be worn to a stub when properly used, but the lopsided broom is no use at all because the chump who handled it always used it one way until the broom became a useless, distorted, lopsided affair, with a permanent list to starboard or port, as the case may be.

To sweep properly is an art, and every all-around outdoor boy and man should learn to sweep and to handle the broom as skillfully as he does his gun or axe. In the first place, turn the broom every time you notice a tendency of the latter to become one-sided, then the broom will wear to a stub and still be of use. In the next place, do not swing the broom up in the air with each sweep and throw the dust up in the clouds, but so sweep that the end of the stroke keeps the broom near the floor or ground.

Now a word about making beds. In all books on woodcraft you are directed to secure balsam boughs from which to make your beds, and there is no better forest bedding than the fragrant balsam boughs, but unfortunately the mountain goose, as the hunters call it, from which you pluck the feathers to make your camp bed, is not to be found in all localities.

A bag filled with dry leaves, dry grass, hay or straw will make a very confortable mattress; but we are not always in the hay and straw belt and dry leaves are sometimes difficult to secure; a scout, however, must learn to make a bed wherever he happens to be. If there happens to be a swale nearby where brakes and ferns grow luxuriantly, one can gather an armful of these, and with them make a mattress. The Interrupted fern, the Cinnamon, the Royal fern, the Lady fern, the Marsh fern and all the larger ferns are useful as material.

A camping party should have their work so divided that each one can immediately start at his own particular job the moment a halt is made. One chops up the firewood and sees that a plentiful supply of firewood is always on hand; usually he carries the water. One makes camp, puts up the tents, clears away the rubbish, fixes the beds, etc., while a third attends strictly to kitchen work, preparing the meals, and washing up the dishes.

With the labor divided in this manner, things run like clock work and camp is always neat and tidy. Roughing it is making the best of it; only a slob and a chump goes dirty and has a sloppy-looking camp. The real old time veteran and sourdough is a model of neatness and order. But a clean, orderly camp is much more important than a clean-faced camper. Some men think so much of themselves and their own personal cleanliness that they forget their duty to the others.   One's duty is about in this proportion: first to the animals if any, secondly to the men, and lastly to oneself.

Before pitching your tent, clear out a space for it to occupy; pick up the stones, rubbish and sticks, rake off the ground with a forked stick.   But do not be rude to your brother, the ground pine; apologize for disturbing it; be gentle with the fronds of the fern; do not tear the trailing arbutus vine up by its roots, or the plant of the almond scented twin flowers; ask pardon of the thallus of the lichen which you are trampling under your feet.   Why?   O! well—because they had first right to the place, and because such little civilities to the natural objects around you put your own mind in accord with nature, and make camping a much more enjoyable affair.

When you feel you are sleeping on the breast of *your mother*, the earth, while *your father*, the sky, with his millions of eyes is watching over you, and that you are surrounded by your brother, the plants, the wilderness is no longer lonesome even to the solitary traveler.

Another reason for taking this point of view is that it has a humanizing effect and tends to prevent one from becoming a wilderness Hun and vandal.   It also not only makes one hesitate to hack the trees unnecessarily, but encourages the camper to take pride in leaving a clean trail.   As my good friend, John Muir, said to me: "The camping trip need not be the longest and most dangerous excursion up to the highest mountain, through the deepest woods or across the wildest torrents, glaciers or deserts, in order to be a happy one; but however short or long, rough or smooth, calm or stormy, it should be one in which the able, fearless camper sees the most, learns the most, loves the most and leaves the cleanest track; whose camp grounds are never marred by anything unsightly, scarred trees or blood spots or bones of animals."

It is not the object of this book to advertise, or even advise the use of any particular type of outfitting apparatus other than the plain, everyday affairs with which all are familiar. What we want to do is to start the reader right, then he may make his own choice, selecting an outfit to suit his own taste. There are no two men, for instance, who will sing the praise of the same sort of a tent, but there is perhaps no camper who has not used, and been very comfortable in, the old style wall tent. It has its disadvantages, and so has a house, a shack or a shanty. As a rule, the old wall tent is too heavy to carry with comfort and very difficult for one man to pitch alone—unless one knows how.

Tent Pegs

Are necessary for almost any kind of a tent; you can buy them at the outfitter's and lose them on the way to camp; they even have iron and steel tent pegs to help make camping expensive, and to scatter through the woods. But if you are a real sourdough you will cut your own tent pegs, shaped according to circumstances and individual taste. Fig. 286 shows the two principal kinds: the fork and the notched tent pegs. For the wall tents one will need a ridge pole (Fig. 288), and two forked sticks, or rods, to support the ridge pole; the forks on these should be snubbed off close so that they will not thrust themselves up against the canvas on the top of the tent and endanger the fabric; these poles should be of a proper height; otherwise if the poles are too long, the tent will not touch the ground at all, or if the poles are too short, the tent will wrinkle all over the ground like a fellow's trousers when his suspenders break.

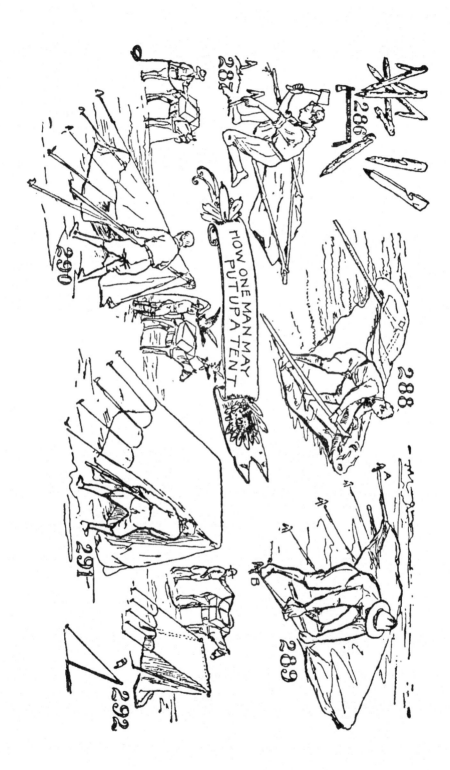

HOW ONE MAN MAY PUT UP A TENT

See that the ground is comparatively level, but with a slant in one direction or another so that water will drain off in case of rain. Never, for instance, pitch your tent in a hollow or basin of ground, unless you want to wake up some night slopping around in a pool of water. Do not pitch your tent near a standing dead tree; it is liable to fall over and crush you in the night. Avoid camping under green trees with heavy dead branches on them. Remember the real camper always has an eye to safety first, not because he is a coward, but because the real camper is as brave a person as you will find anywhere, and no real brave person believes in the carelessness which produces accidents. Do not pitch your tent over protruding stones which will make stumbling-blocks for you on which to stub your toes at night, or torture you when you spread your blankets over them to sleep. Use common sense, use gumption. Of course, we all know that *it hurts one's head to think*, but we must all try it, nevertheless, if we are going to live in the big outdoors.

At a famous military academy the splendid cavalrymen gave a brilliant exhibition of putting up wall tents; it required four men to put up each tent. Immediately following this some of the scouts took the same tents, with one scout to each tent, and in less time than the cavalrymen took for the same job, the twelve year old boys, single-handed, put up the same tents.

How to Pitch and Ditch Single-handed

Spread out your tent all ready to erect, put your ridge pole and your two uprights in place, and then drive some tent stakes, using the flat of your axe with which to drive them, so that you will not split the tops of the stakes (Fig. 287); drive the two end stakes A and B (Fig. 289) at an angle to the ends of the tent. After the tent stakes are arranged in a row, like the ones in Fig. 289, adjust the forks of the uprights two inches from the ends of the ridge pole (Fig. 288), then make fast the two extreme end guy ropes A and B to the tent pegs; the others are unimportant for the present; after that is done, raise one tent pole part of the way up (Fig. 290), then push the other part of the way up (Fig. 291); gradually adjust these things until the strain is even upon your guy ropes. You will now find that your tent will stand alone, because the weight is pulling against your guy ropes (Fig. 292). This will hold your tent steady until you can make fast the guy ropes to the pegs upon the other side, not too tightly, because you need slack to straighten up your tent poles.

Next see that the back guy pole is perpendicular, after which it is a very easy matter to straighten up the front pole and adjust the guy rope so that it will stand stiff as in Fig. 293.

Remember, when you are cutting the ridge poles and the uprights, to select fairly straight sticks, and they should be as free as possible from rough projections, which might injure the canvas; also the poles should be as stiff as possible so as not to sag or cause the roof to belly.

DITCHING

Just as soon as your tent is erected and you feel like resting, get busy on ditching; no matter how dry the weather may be at the time, put a ditch around the tent that will drain the water away from your living place. There is no positive rule for digging this ditch; it varies according to surface of ground, but the gutter should be so made that the water will run away from the tents and not to it, or stand around it (Fig. 294). Fig. 295 shows how to make a tent by

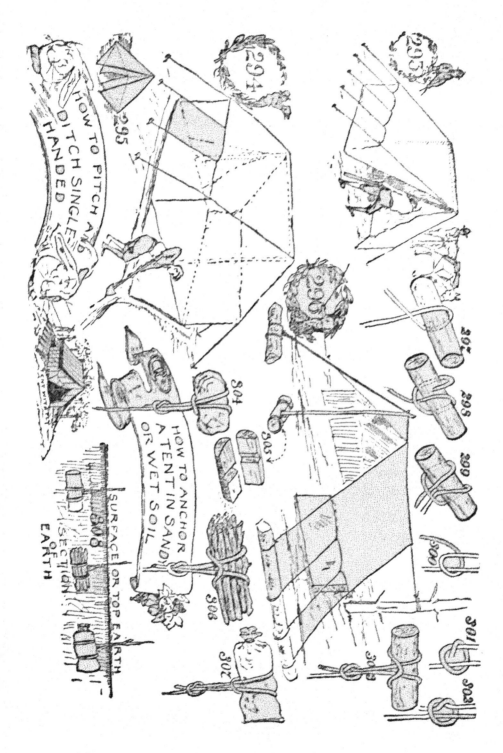

HOW TO PITCH AND
DITCH SINGLE-
HANDED

294

295

HOW TO ANCHOR
A TENT IN SAND
OR WET SOIL

SURFACE OR TOP EARTH
SECTION OF EARTH

14

folding a floor cloth or piece of tarpaulin; of course it must have a tent pole to support the top, and the floor pieces may be drawn together in the center. Make one out of a piece of writing paper and you will learn how to do it, because although the paper is small, the folds would be just the same as if it was as large as a church.

In sandy or soft ground it often taxes one's ingenuity to supply anchors for one's tent; an anchor is a weight of some sort to which the guy ropes may be attached. Fig 296 shows a tent anchored by billets of wood; these are all supposed to be buried in the ground as in Fig. 308, and the ground trampled down over and above them to keep them safe in their graves. Fig. 297 shows the first throw in the anchor hitch, Fig. 298 the second throw, and Fig. 299 the complete hitch for the anchor. Fig. 303 shows the knot by which the anchor rope is tied to the main line. Figs. 300, 301 and 302 show the detail of tying this knot, which is simplicity itself, when you know how, like most knots. Fig. 303 shows the anchor hitch complete.

Stones, bundles of fagots; or bags of sand all make useful anchors; Fig. 304 is a stone; Fig. 305 are half billets of wood, Fig. 306 shows fagots of wood, Fig. 307 a bag of sand. All may be used to anchor your tent in the sands or loose ground.

SHEARS, GINS OR TRIPODS

Are the names used for different forms of rustic supports for the tents. Fig. 312 shows the ordinary shears, Fig. 313 shows the tent supported by shears; you will also note that the guy ropes for the tent (Fig. 313) are made fast to a rod instead of to the pegs in the ground. This has many advantages, because of the tendency of the rope to tighten or shrink whenever it becomes wet, which often makes it necessary for a fellow to get up in the night to adjust the guy ropes and redrive the pegs. When the rain is pouring down, the thunder crashing and the lightning flashing, it is no fun to go poking around on the wet ground in one's nightie in order that the tent pegs may not be pulled out of the ground by the shrinking ropes, and the cold mass of wet canvas allowed to fall upon one's head. It is always necessary to loosen and tighten the guy ropes according to the weather; naturally the longer the guy ropes are the more they will shrink and the more they will stretch as the weather varies. To prevent this, lay a rod over the ends of the guy rope between the pegs and the tent (Fig. 316A) and it will be an automatic adjuster. When the ropes are dry and stretch, the weight of this pole will hold them down and keep them taut; when the guy ropes shrink they will lift the pole, but the latter will keep the tension on the ropes and keep them adjusted. The arrangement of Fig. 313 has the advantage of making a clothes rack for your bed clothes when you wish to air them, while the weight of the suspended log keeps the tension on the ropes equalized. Fig. 314 shows the shears made by the use of forked sticks. Figs. 315 and 318 show the ridge pole supported by shears, and the ridge poles supported by forked sticks; the advantage of the shears in Fig. 315 is that it gives a clear opening to the tent. Fig. 316 shows an exterior ridge pole supported by shears to which the top of the tent is made fast. Fig. 317 is the same without the tent. Fig. 318 shows the famous Vreeland tent; in this case the ridge pole is supported by a crotched upright stick, but may be equally well supported by the shears as in Fig. 315. Fig. 319 shows the gin or tripod made by binding the three sticks together. Fig. 320 shows the same effect made by the use of the forked sticks; these are useful in pitching wigwams or tepees.

COMMON TENTS OF THE OPEN COUNTRY

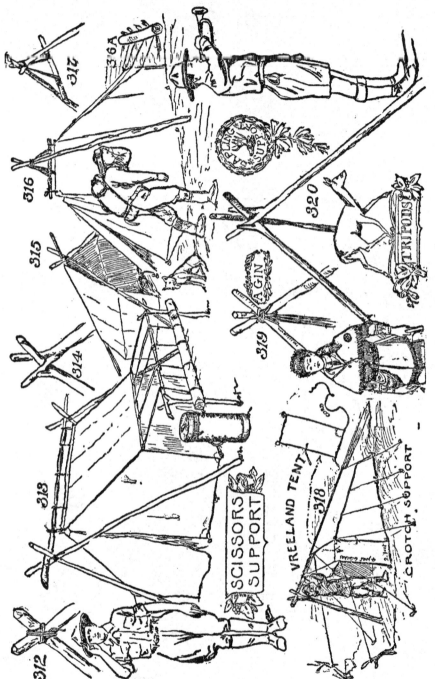

SOME POPULAR TENTS

Fig. 309 shows some of the ordinary forms of tents, the wall tent, the Baker tent and the canoe tent. Fig. 310 shows a tent with a fly extending out in front, thus giving the piazza or front porch. In the background is a tepee tent. Fig. 311 shows two small Baker tents in the background, and the Dan Beard tent in the foreground. These comprise the principal forms, but the open-front tents to-day are much in vogue with the campers. A mosquito netting in front will keep out the insects and allow the air to come in freely, whereas the old-fashioned way of closing the tent flap stops circulation of air and makes conditions as bad as that of a closed room in a big house, and the air becomes as foul as it did in the little red school houses and does now in the Courts of Justice, jails and other places of entertainment.

CHAPTER XII

AXE AND SAW

CHAPTER XII

AXE AND SAW

To all good, loyal Americans, the axe is almost a sacred tool, for our greatest American, Abraham Lincoln, was one of our greatest axemen. When he was President of the United States he used to exercise by chopping wood, then laughingly extended his arm holding the axe in a horizontal position by the extreme end of the handle. This he would do without a tremor of the muscle or movement of the axe—some stunt! Try it and see if you can do it!

The American Indians, and practically all savages, used stone and bone implements, and with such implements the Redmen were wont to build the most beautiful of all crafts, the birch bark canoe. If an American Indian produced such wonders with implements made of stones, flint and bones, a good red-blooded American boy should be able to do the same with a sharp axe; therefore it should not only be his pleasure but his duty to learn to be a skillful axeman.

Brother Jonathan, the imaginary character who represented the American people, was almost invariably pictured with a jack-knife whittling a stick, because all early Americans were skillful in the use of the jack-knife, but they were also skilled in the use of the axe, and every boy of twelve years of age knew how to handle an axe.

IMPORTANCE OF THE AXE

While lecturing at the Teachers' College, Columbia University, I was asked to give a demonstration of the use of the axe. It then and there suddenly occurred to me that if these grown men needed and asked for instructions in the use of this typical American tool, a talk on the same subject would be welcomed by the American boys.

The axe is the one necessary tool of the woodsmen; the axe occupies the same position to the wilderness man that the chest of tools does to the carpenter; with the axe the woodsman cuts his firewood; with the axe he makes his traps; with the axe he splits the shakes, clapboards, slabs and shingles from the balsam tree, or other wood which splits readily, and with the shakes, clapboards, or slabs he shingles the roof of his hogan, his barabara, or makes the framework to his sod shack or his dugout, or with them builds the foundation of a bogken. With his axe he cuts the birch for his birch bark pontiac, for his lean-to or his log cabin. Without an axe it is most difficult for one to even build a raft or to fell a tree to get the birch bark for one's canoe, or to "fall" the tree to make a dugout canoe. A tree may be felled by fire, as the Indians of old used to "fall" them, but this takes a wearisome time.

The Kind of Axe to Use

When bound for a real camp, take along with you a real axe. Never take an axe which is too large and heavy for you to swing with comfort. It is also best to avoid an axe which is too light, as with such a tool you must use too much labor to cut the wood. You should select your own axe according to your strength. Pick up the axe, go through the motions of chopping and see if it feels right, if its balance suits you; hold up the axe and sight along the top of the handle as you would along the barrel of a gun to see that your handle is not warped.

Axes may be had of weight and size to suit one's taste. In New England they use short-handled axes which are not popular in the woods. The axe handles should be well seasoned, second growth hickory; a ¼ axe has a 19-inch handle and weighs two pounds. A ½ axe has a 24-inch handle and weighs two and a half pounds. A ¾ axe has a 28-inch handle and weighs three pounds. A full axe has a 36-inch handle and weighs five pounds.

Probably the best axe for camp work, when you must carry the axe on your back, is one with a 30-inch second growth hickory handle, weight about two and three-quarter pounds, or somewhere between two and three pounds. A light axe of this kind will cut readily and effectively provided it has a slender bit; that is, that it does not sheer off too bluntly towards the cutting edge. When you look at the top of such an axe and it appears slender and not bulky, it will cut well and can be wielded by a boy and is not too light for a man (Fig. 322).

Fig. 321 shows the long-handled Hudson Bay axe used much in the North country. It is made after the tomahawk form to save weight, but the blade is broad, you notice, to give a wide cutting edge. The trouble with this axe is that it is too light for satisfactory work. Fig. 323 shows a belt axe of a modified tomahawk shape, only three of which are in existence; one was in the possession of the late Colonel Roosevelt, one in the possession of a famous English author, and one in the possession of the writer. These axes were made for the gentlemen to whom they were presented by the President of a great tool works; they are made of the best gray steel and are beautiful tools. Fig. 324 is an ordinary belt axe practically the same as those used by the Boy Scouts. When it was proposed to arm the Boy Scouts with guns, the writer put in strenuous objections and suggested belt axes in place of guns; the matter of costume and arms was finally referred to him as a committee of one. The uniform was planned after that of the Scouts of the Boy Pioneers of America, and the belt axe adopted is the same as that carried by the Scouts of the Sons of Daniel Boone, which axes are modelled after Daniel Boone's own tomahawk. Fig. 325 is a very heavy axe.

A Word About Swinging the Axe

Grasp the axe with the left hand, close to the end of the handle, even closer than is shown in the diagram (Fig. 326); with the right hand grasp the handle close to the head of the axe, then bring the axe up over your shoulder and as you strike the blow, allow the right hand to slide down naturally (Fig. 327), close to the left hand; learn to reverse, that is, learn to grasp the lower end of the handle with the right hand and the left hand near the top, so as to swing the axe from the left shoulder down, as easily as from the right shoulder.

To be a real axeman, a genuine dyed-in-the-wool, blown-in-the-glass type, each time you make a stroke with the axe you must emit the breath from your lungs with a noise like Huh! That, you know, sounds very professional and will duly impress the other boys when they watch you chop, besides which it always seems to really help the force of the blow.

How to Remove a Broken Axe Handle

It was from a colored rail splitter from Virginia, who worked for the writer, that the latter learned how to burn out the broken end of the handle from the axe head. Bury the blade of your axe in the moist earth and build a fire over the protruding butt (Fig. 328); the moist earth will prevent the heat from spoiling the temper of your axe blade while the heat from the fire will char and burn the wood so that it can easily be removed.

If you are using a double-bitted axe, that is, one of those very useful but villainous tools with two cutting edges, and the handle breaks off, make a shallow trench in the dirt, put the moist soil over each blade, leaving a hollow in the middle where the axe handle comes and build your fire over this hollow (Fig. 329).

To Tighten the Axe Head

If your axe handle is dry and the head loosens, soak it over night and the wood will swell and tighten the head. Scoutmaster Fitzgerald of New York says, "Quite a number of scouts have trouble with the axe slipping off the helve and the first thing they do is to drive a nail which only tends to split the helve and make matters worse. I have discovered a practical way of fixing this. You will note that a wire passes over the head of the axe in the helve in the side view. Then in the cross-section in the copper wire is twisted and a little staple driven in to hold it in place." This may answer for a belt axe but the hole in the handle will weaken it and would not be advisable for a large axe (Fig. 330).

Accidents

We have said that the axe is a chest of tools, but it is a dangerous chest of tools. While aboard a train coming from one of the big lumber camps, the writer was astonished to find that although there were but few sick men aboard, there were many, many wounded men in the car and none, that he

15

could find, wounded by falling trees; all were wounded by the axe itself or by fragments of knots and sticks flying from blows of the axe and striking the axeman in the eyes or other tender places.

You Must Supply the Brains

I have often warned my young friends to use great care with firearms, because firearms are made for the express purpose of killing. A gun, having no brains of its own, will kill its owner, his friends, his brother or sister, mother or father, just as quickly and as surely as it will kill a moose, a bear or a panther. Therefore it is necessary for the gunner to supply the brains for his gun.

The same is true with the axeman. Edged tools are made for the express purpose of cutting, and they will cut flesh and bone as quickly and neatly as they will cut wood, unless the user is skillful in the use of his tool; that is, unless he supplies the brains which the tools themselves lack.

So you see that it is "up to you" boys to supply the brains for your axes, and when you do that, that is, when you acquire the skill in the use, and judgment in the handling, you will avoid painful and may be dangerous or fatal accidents, and at the same time you will experience great joy in the handling of your axe. Not only this but you will acquire muscle and health in this most vigorous and manly exercise.

We are not telling all this to frighten the reader but to instil into his mind a proper respect for edged tools, especially the axe.

Etiquette of the Axe

1. An axe to be respected must be sharp and no one who has any ambition to be a pioneer, a sportsman or a scout, should carry a dull axe, or an axe with the edge

nicked like a saw blade. It may interest the reader to know that the pencil I am using with which to make these notes was sharpened with my camp axe.

2. No one but a duffer and a chump will use another man's axe without that other man's willing permission.

3. It is as bad form to ask for the loan of a favorite axe as it is to ask for the loan of a sportsman's best gun or pet fishing rod or toothbrush.

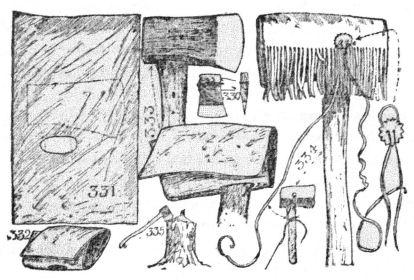

AXES AND SHEATHS

4. To turn the edge or to nick another man's axe is a very grave offense.

5. Keep your own axe sharp and clean, do not use it to cut any object lying on the ground where there is danger of the blade of the axe going through the object and striking a stone; do not use it to cut roots of trees or bushes for the same reason. Beware of knots in hemlock wood and in cold weather beware of knots of any kind.

When not in use an axe should have its blade sheathed in leather (Figs. 331, 332, 333 and 334), or it should be struck into a log or stump (Fig. 335). It should never be left upon the ground or set up against a tree to endanger the legs and feet of the camper. Fig. 341 shows how a firewood hod is made and used.

How to Sharpen Your Axe

On the trail we have no grindstones, and often have recourse to a file with which to sharpen our axe; sometimes we use a whetstone for the purpose. New axes are not always as sharp as one would wish; in that case if we use a grindstone to put on an edge we must be sure to keep the grindstone wet in the first place, and in the second place we must be careful not to throw the edge of the blade out of line. When this occurs it will cause a "binding strain" on the blade which tends to stop the force of the blow. If the edges are at all out of line, the probabilities are one will knock a half moon out of the blade in the first attempt to cut frozen timber. The best axe in the world, with an edge badly out of line, cannot stand the strain of a blow on hard frozen wood. While grinding the axe take a sight along the edge every once in a while to see if it is true.

The Best Time to Cut or Prune Trees

Is when the sap is dormant, which I will explain for my younger readers is that time of year when the tree is not full of juice. The reason for this is that when the sap or juice is in the wood when cut, it will ferment, bubble and fizzle the same as sweet cider or grape juice will ferment, and the fermentation will take all the "life" out of the lumber and give it a tendency to decay; again to translate for my younger readers, such wood will rot quicker than wood cut at the proper season of the year.

WOOD HODS

341

337

338

336

339

CHOPPING BLOCKS

340

DONT

With pine trees, however, this is not always the case, because the pitchy nature of the sap of the pine prevents it from fermenting like beech sap; in fact, the pitch acts as a preservative and mummifies, so to speak, the wood. Pine knots will last for a hundred years lying in the soft, moist ground and for aught I know, longer, because they are fat with pitch and the pitch prevents decay.

Beech when cut in June is unfit for firewood the following winter, but authorities say that the same trees cut in August and left with the branches still on them for twenty or thirty days, will make firmer and "livelier" timber than that cut under any other conditions.

An expert lumberman in ten minutes' time will cut down a hardwood tree one foot in diameter, and it will not take him over four minutes to cut down a softwood tree of the same size.

Clear Away Everything

Before attempting to chop down a tree; in fact, before attempting to chop anything, be careful to see that there are no clothes lines overhead, if you are chopping in your back-yard, or if you are chopping in the forests see that there are no vines, twigs, or branches within swing of your axe. By carefully removing all such things you will remove one of the greatest causes of accidents in the wilderness, for as slight a thing as a little twig can deflect, that is, turn, the blade of your axe from its course and cause the loss of a toe, a foot, or even a leg. This is the reason that swamping is the most dangerous part of the lumberman's work.

How to "Fall" a Tree

If the tree, in falling, must pass between two other trees where there is danger of its "hanging," so cut your kerf that the tree in falling will strike the ground nearest the smallest of the trees, or nearest the one furthest away. Then, as the tree falls, and brushes the side of the smallest tree or the one furthest away, it will bounce away, thus giving the fallen tree an opportunity to bump its way down to the place on the ground selected for it, in place of hanging by its bough in the boughs of other trees.

Do not try to "fall" a tree between two others that are standing close together; it cannot be successfully done, for the tops of the three trees will become interlaced, and you will find it very difficult and hazardous work to attempt to free your fallen tree from its entanglement; probably it cannot be done without cutting one or both of the other trees down. The truth is, one must mix brains with every stroke of the axe or one will get into trouble.

Where possible select a tree that may be made to fall in an open space where the prostrate trunk can be easily handled. Cut your kerf on the side toward the landing place, let the notch go half-way or a trifle more through the trunk. Make the notch or kerf as wide as the radius, that is, half the diameter of the tree trunk (Fig. 344), otherwise you will have your axe pinched or wedged before you have the kerf done and will find it necessary to enlarge your notch or kerf. Score first at the top part of the proposed notch, then at the bottom, making as big chips as possible, and hew out the space between, cutting the top parts of the notch at an angle but the bottom part nearly horizontal. When this notch or kerf is cut to half or a little more than half of the diameter of the tree, cut another notch upon the opposite side of the tree at a point a few inches higher than the notch already cut; when this notch is cut far enough the tree will begin to tremble **and crack to warn** you to step to one side. Don't get behind the tree; it may kick and kill you; step to one side and watch the tree as it falls; there are many things that may deflect it in falling, and one's safety lies in being alert and watching it fall. Also keep your eye aloft to watch for limbs which may break off and come down with sufficient force to disable you; accidents of this kind frequently happen, but seldom or never happen where the axeman uses common sense or due caution.

How to Trim or Swamp

After a tree is felled, the swampers take charge of it and cut away all the branches, leaving the clean log for the teamsters to "snake." They do the swamping by striking the lower side of the branch with the blade of the axe, the side towards the root of the tree, what might be called the underside, and chopping upwards towards the top of the tree. Small branches will come off with a single blow of the axe.

When the tree has been swamped and the long trunk lies naked on the turf, it will, in all probability, be necessary to cut it into logs of required lengths. If the trunk is a thick one it is best to cut it by standing on the tree trunk with legs apart (Fig. 336), and chopping between one's feet, making the kerf equal to the diameter of the log. Do this for two reasons: it is much easier to stand on a log and cut it in two that way than to cut it part the way through the top side, and then laboriously roll it over and cut from the underside; also when you make the notch wide enough you can cut all the way through the log without wedging your axe. To split up the log you should have

A Beetle or Mall,

A thing usually to be found among the tools in the back-woodsman's hut and permanent camps; of course we do not

take the time to make them for an overnight camp or a
temporary camping place, but they are very handy at a
stationary camp. To make one select a hardwood tree, which,
when stripped of its bark will measure about five inches in
diameter. The tree selected should not be one that would
split easily but may be a young oak, beech or hickory, which
with the bark on is six or seven inches in diameter at the butt.
In chopping this tree down leave a stump tall enough from
which to fashion your beetle, and while the stump is still
standing hew the top part until you have a handle scant two
feet in length, leaving for the hammer head, so to speak, a
butt of ten inches, counting from the part where the roots
join the trunk. Before cutting the stump off above the
ground, dig all around the roots, carefully scraping away all
stones and pebbles, then cut the roots off close up to the
stump, for this is the hardest part of the wood and makes the
best mall head (Fig. 337).

How to Make the Gluts or Wedges

Farmers claim that the best wedges are made of applewood, or locust wood; never use green wedges if seasoned
ones may be obtained, for one seasoned wedge is worth many
green ones. In the north woods, or, in fact, in any woods,
applewood cannot be obtained, but dogwood and ironwood
make good substitutes even when used green (Figs. 338
and 357).

How to Harden Green Wood

Many of the Southern Indians in the early history of
America tipped their arrows with bits of cane; these green
arrow points they hardened by slightly charring them with
the hot ashes of the fire. Gluts may be hardened in the
same manner; do not burn them; try to heat them just suffi-

ciently to force the sap out and harden the surface. Where dogwood, ironwood and applewood are not to be obtained, make your gluts of what is at hand; that is true woodcraft (Fig. 337).

A year or two ago, while trailing a moose, we ran across the ruins of a lumber camp that had been wiped out by fire, and here we picked up half a dozen axe heads among the moose tracks. These axe heads we used as gluts to split our wood as long as we remained in that camp, and by their aid we built a shack of board rived from balsam logs.

Fig. 341 shows how to make and how to use firewood hods on farms or at permanent camps.

How to Make a Chopping Block

After you have cut the crotch and trimmed it down into the form of Fig. 339, you may find it convenient to flatten the thing on one side. This you do by hewing and scoring; that is, by cutting a series of notches all of the same depth, and then splitting off the wood between the notches, as one would in making a puncheon (Fig: 342). (A puncheon is a log flattened on one or both sides.) With this flattened crotch one may, by sinking another flattened log in the earth and placing the chopping block on top, have a chopping block like that shown in Fig. 343. Or one may take the crotch, spike a piece of board across as in Fig. 339 and use that, and the best chopping block or crotch block is the one shown in Fig. 339, with the puncheon or slab spiked onto the ends of the crotch. In this case the two ends of the crotch should be cut off with a saw, if you have one, so as to give the proper flat surface to which to nail the slab. Then the kindling wood may be split without danger to yourself or the edge of the hatchet.

Chop it the Right Way

If you are using an ordinary stick of wood for a chopping block, and the stick you are about to chop rests solidly on top of the block *where the axe strikes* it will cut all right, but if you strike where the stick does not touch the chopping block the blow will stun the hand holding the stick in a very disagreeable manner. If you hold your stick against the chopping block with your foot, there is always danger of cutting off your toe; if you hold the stick with your hand and strike it with the axe, there is danger of cutting off your fingers. When I say there is danger I mean it. One of our scouts cut his thumb off, another cut off one finger, and one of my friends in the North woods of Canada cut off his great toe. In hunting for Indian relics in an old camping cave in Pennsylvania, my companion, Mr. Elmer Gregor, made the gruesome find of a dried human finger near the embers of an ancient campfire, telling the story of a camping accident ages ago, but evidently after white man's edged tools were introduced.

If you have no chopping block and wish to cut your firewood into smaller pieces, you can hold the stick safely with the hand if you use the axe as shown in Fig. 345. This will give you as a result two sticks, and the upper one will have some great splinters.

How to Split Kindling Wood

When splitting wood for the fire or kindling, make the first blow as in Fig. 346, and the second blow in the same place, but a trifle slanting as in Fig. 347; the slanting blow wedges the wood apart and splits it. If the wood is small and splits readily, the slanting blow may be made first. These things can only be indicated to the readers because there are so many circumstances which govern the case. If there is a knot in the wood, strike the axe right over the knot as in Figs. 348 and 349.

If you are chopping across the grain do not strike perpendicularly as in Fig. 350, because if the wood is hard the axe will simply bounce back, but strike a slanting blow as in Fig. 351, and the axe blade will bite deeply into the wood; again let us caution you that if you put too much of a slant on your axe in striking the wood, it will cut out a shallow chip without materially impeding the force of the blow, and your axe will swing around to the peril of yourself or anyone else within reach; again this is a thing which you must learn to practice.

In using the chopping block be very careful not to put a log in front of the crotch as in Fig. 340, and then strike a heavy blow with the axe, for the reason that if you split the wood with the first blow your axe handle will come down heavily and suddenly upon the front log, and no matter how good a handle it may be, it will break into fragments, as the writer has discovered by sad experience. A lost axe handle in the woods is a severe loss, and one to be avoided, for although a makeshift handle may be fashioned at camp, it never answers the purpose as well as the skillfully and artistically made handle which comes with the axe.

HOLDERS OR SAW BUCKS FOR LOGS

Select two saplings about five inches in diameter at the butts, bore holes near the butts about six inches from the end for legs, make a couple of stout legs about the size of an old-fashioned drey pin, and about twenty inches long, split the ends carefully, sufficiently to insert wedges therein, then drive the wedge and ends into the hole bored for the purpose. When the sticks are driven home the wedge will hold them in place. You now have a couple of "straddle bugs," that is, poles, the small ends of which rest upon the ground and the butt ends supported by two legs. In the top of the poles bore a number of holes for pins, make your pins a little longer than the diameter of the log you intend to saw; the pins are used exactly like the old-fashioned drey pins, that is, you roll the log up the incline to the two straddle bugs and hold the logs in place by putting pins in the nearest holes. Of course, the pins should work easily in and out of the holes (Fig. 357).

With such an arrangement one man can unaided easily roll a log two feet in diameter up upon the buck; the log is then in a position to be cut up with a cross-cut saw (Fig. 357). Another form of sawbuck may be made of a puncheon stool (Fig. 358), with holes bored diagonally in the top for the insertion of pins with which to hold the log in place while it is being sawed. But with this sawbuck one cannot use as heavy logs as with the first one because of the difficulty in handling them.

I have just returned from a trip up into the woods where they still use the primitive pioneer methods of handling and cutting timber, and I note up there in Pike County, Pennsylvania, they make the sawbuck for logs by using a log of wood about a foot in diameter and boring holes diagonally through the log near each end (Fig. 359); through these holes they drive the legs so that the ends of them protrude at the top and form a crotch to hold the wood to be sawed. The sawbuck is about ten or twelve feet long; consequently, in order to provide for shorter logs there are two sets of pegs driven in holes bored for the purpose between the ends of the buck.

The Parbuckle

When one person is handling a heavy log it is sometimes difficult, even with the lumberman's canthook, to roll it, but if a loop is made in a rope and placed over a stump or a heavy stone (Fig. 360), and the ends run under the log, even a boy can roll quite a heavy piece of timber by pulling on the ends of the rope (Fig. 360).

To Split a Log

The method used by all woodsmen in splitting a log is the same as used by quarrymen in splitting bluestone, with this difference: the quarryman hunts for a natural seam in the stone and drives the wedge in the seam, while the lumberman makes a seam in the form of a crack in the log by a blow from his axe. In the crack he drives the wedge (Figs. 352 and 353). But if the log is a long one he must lengthen the crack or seam by driving other wedges or gluts (Fig. 353), or he may do it by using two or more axes (Fig. 352).

If he wishes to split the logs up into shakes, clapboards or splits, he first halves the log, that is, splitting it across from A to B (Fig. 356), and then quarters it by splitting from C to D, and so on until he has the splits of the required size.

A Sawpit

In the olden times, the good old times, when people did things with their own hands, and thus acquired great skill with the use of their hands, boards were sawed out from the logs by placing the log on a scaffolding over a sawpit (Fig. 361)

In the good old times, the slow old times, the safe old times, a house was not built in a week or a month; the timber was well seasoned, well selected, and in many cases such

16

houses are standing to-day! On the next block where I live and from where I am writing, and across the street, there stands a house still occupied which was built in 1661. It is the house that Fox, the Quaker, was quartered in when he was preaching under the spreading oaks on Long Island. The timbers of this house are still sound and strong, although the woodwork in nearby modern houses is decaying.

In the mountains of Kentucky and Tennessee they still use the sawpit, and the logs are held in place by jacks (Fig. 355), which are branches of trees hooked over the log and the longest fork of the branch is then sprung under the supporting cross-piece (Fig. 361).

Of course, the boy readers of this book are not going to be top sawyers or make use of a sawpit; that is a real man's work, a big HE man's work, but the boys of to-day should know all these things; it is part of history and they can better understand the history of our own country when they know how laboriously, cheerily and cheerfully their ancestors worked to build their own homesteads, and in the building of their own homesteads they unconsciously built that character of which their descendants are so proud; also they built up a physique that was healthy, and a sturdy body for which their descendants are particularly thankful, because good health and good physique are hereditary, that is, boys, if your parents, your grandparents and your great grandparents were all healthy, wholesome people, you started your life as a healthy, wholesome child.

In this chapter the writer has emphasized the danger of edged tools for beginners, but he did that to make them careful in the use of the axe, not to discourage them in acquiring skill with it. We must remember that there is nothing in life that is not dangerous, and the greatest danger of all is not firearms, is not edged tools, is not wild beasts, is not tornadoes or earthquakes, avalanches or floods, but it is LUXURY; expressed in boy language, it is ice cream, soda water, candy, servants and automobiles; it is everything which tends to make a boy dependent upon others and soft in mind and muscle and to make him a sissy. But hardship, in the sense of undergoing privation and doing hard work like chopping trees and sawing logs, makes a rugged body, a clean, healthy mind, and gives long life. So, boys, don't be afraid to build your own little shack, shanty or shelter, to chop the kindling wood for your mother, to split up logs for the fun of doing it, or just to show that you know how. Don't be afraid to be a real pioneer so that you may grow up to be a real Abe Lincoln!

If I am talking to men, they need no detailed definition of luxury; they know all about it, its cause and its effect; they also know that luxury kills a race and hardship preserves a race. The American boy should be taught to love hardship for hardship's sake, and then the Americans as a race will be a success, and a lasting one.

CHAPTER XIII

COUNCIL GROUNDS AND FIRES

CHEROKEE INDIAN COUNCIL BARBECUE
CAMP MEETING COUNCIL GROUND
THE INDIAN PALISADED COUNCIL FIRE
INDIAN LEGENDS OF THE FIRE
STEALING THE FIRE FROM THE SUN-MAIDENS OF THE EAST
MYTHS OF THE MEWAN INDIANS
TOTEMS OF THE FOUR WINDS, FOUR MOUNTAINS AND FOUR
    POINTS OF THE COMPASS
IMPRACTICAL COUNCIL FIRES
ADVANTAGES OF THE OVAL COUNCIL GROUND
HOW TO MAKE AN ELLIPSE
HOW TO DIVIDE THE COUNCIL GROUND IN FOUR COURTS
COUNCIL CEREMONIES
GHOST WALK AND PATH OF KNOWLEDGE
WHAT THE DIFFERENT COLORS STAND FOR
PATRIOTISM, POETRY AND AMERICANISM
CAMP MEETING TORCH FIRES

CHAPTER XIII

COUNCIL GROUNDS AND FIRES

Now that we have learned about the serious part of camping, hiking and woodcraft, about fire-building, cooking and axe work, we will leave the long trail and the hard trail and dump our duffel bag in a recreation camp, a Boy Scout camp, a Y. M. C. A. camp, or a school camp, and after we have pitched our tent and arranged our cot to suit our own convenience and everything is ship-shape for the night, it is time for us to get busy on our "good turn" and do something for the crowd.

Like the great Boy Scout Movement, the council fire is also a product of America. The council fires were burning all over this land when Columbus discovered America. It was around the council fires that the Indians gathered in solemn conclave to consult and discuss the affairs of their tribes.

Originally the council ground was surrounded by a palisade; that is, the fire was in the center of a circular fort. Around this fire the old men of the tribe made their eloquent addresses; also around this fire the warriors danced the scalp dance, the corn dance, the buffalo dance, and all their various religious dances.

Later the Cherokee Indians changed the council fire into a barbecue, where they roasted whole beefs in pits of glowing coals. This custom was adopted by the politicians in Kentucky, and the Kentucky barbecues became very famous; they were what might be called a by-product of the old Indian council fires and a European feast combined. But in 1799 the old Indian council fires became camp meetings, and around the blazing fagots the pioneers gathered to engage in religious revivals. It was at one of these meetings that Daniel Boone's great friend, Simon Kenton, was converted and became a Methodist.

The camp meetings were originated by two brothers by the name of McGee. Bill McGee was a Presbyterian, and John McGee a Methodist minister. They came to Kentucky from West Tennessee. John McGee was such a great backwoods preacher (a pioneer Billy Sunday) that he drew immense crowds of buckskin-clad men, each of whom carried a cow's horn powder flask and a long barreled rifle.

The small buildings used for churches in the pioneer settlements could not hold the crowd, so they gathered around blazing council fires, and from this beginning came the great religious revival which swept the border with a wave of religious enthusiasm.

It is a far call back to the old Indian council fire, and the blazing council fires of the pioneer camp meetings, but to-day all over this land we are holding similar council fires, many of them conducted with much ceremony, and not a few with religious fervor. The summer hotels have their council fires; the great Camp Fire Club of America, composed of all the famous big game hunters, have lately bought a tract of land for the purpose of holding their council fires in the open, and the writer interrupted the writing of this chapter to attend one of the club's council fires. The military schools are holding council fires, and everywhere the Boy Scouts have their council fires blazing; even the girls have fallen in line, and this is as it should be, Therefore it is time that some regular plan was made for these assemblies, and some suggestion of ceremony and some meaning given to the council grounds.

THE INDIAN ORIGINS

We have searched the legends of the Red Man for suggestions, and from various sources have learned that the Indian had a general belief that at the north there is a yellow or black mountain, at the east there is a white mountain of light, at the south there is a red mountain, and at the west there is a blue mountain. At the east and west there are also holes in the sky, through which the sun comes to light us by day, and through which the sun disappears so that we may sleep by night. That is news to most of my readers, but not to the Red Men.

In the "Dawn of the World," Dr. C. Hart Merriam gives a collection of "The Myths and Weird Tales told by the Mewan Indians of California," which are full of poetry and suggestions useful for the council fire work.

It seems that when the white-footed mouse man, and some other of the animal people, were trying to steal the sun, or the fire from which the sun was made, the robin man, Wit-tab-bah, suspected these visitors to be sort of German spies, and so he hovered over the fire, spreading his wings and tail to protect it. Now if you don't believe this you look at the robin's breast and you will see that he still carries the red marks of the fire, which is proof enough for anyone; hence we will give the fire-keeper for our council the name of Wit-tab-bah, the robin.

Since the north is presided over by the totem of the mountain lion, or panther, we will give the officer occupying that court the Indian name of the mountain lion, He-le-jah. The totem of the east is the white timber wolf, Too-le-ze; the color of that court is white, representing light. The totem of the south court is the badger; the color is red and the

Indian name is Too-winks. The color of the west court is blue and the totem is the bear; Kor-le is the Indian name of the bear, and the title of the officer presiding over the blue totem.

The golden or yellow court is the throne of the presiding officer, the scoutmaster of the troop, the headmaster of the school, the gangmaster of your gang, the campmaster of your camp, or the captain of your team. The second in command occupies the white court, the third the red court, and the fourth the blue court. If your council is a military school the commandant occupies the yellow court, the lieutenant-colonel the white court, the major the red court and the first captain the blue court. Now that you have that straight in your heads we will proceed to lay out the court.

The author is aware of the fact that the general reader may be more interested in scout camping, summer camping, and recreation camps than in real wilderness work, but he has tried to impress upon the boys and girls, too, for that matter, the fact that the knowledge of real wilderness work will make even the near-at-home camping easier for them, and very much more interesting; it will also cause them to enjoy the council fire better and have a greater appreciation for everything pertaining to outdoor life. The wilderness campfire over which the solitary explorer or hunter hovers, or around which a group of hunters assemble and spin their yarns, magnified and enlarged to a big blazing fire becomes the council fire around which gather all the members of a recreation camp, the pupils of an outdoor school, a troop or many troops of Boy Scouts; therefore we have given the council fire serious study, because the most inconvenient as well as the most romantic place to talk is at

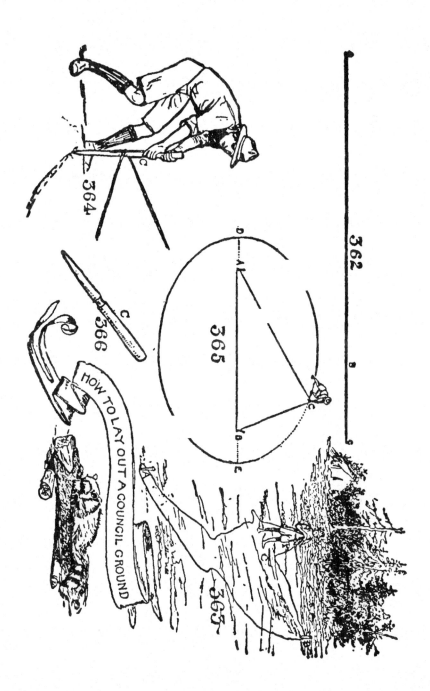

362

364

365

366

363

HOW TO LAY OUT A COUNCIL GROUND

The Council Fire

There could be no more impractical plan for a place to speak than a circle with a big fire in the middle of it, and that is the plan of all the council grounds. The audience must be seated on the circumference of the circle, and the Master of Ceremonies must stand necessarily with his face to the fire and his back to part of his audience, or his back to the fire and consequently also to the part of the audience on the other side of the fire. Having had occasion over and over again to address the scouts at a council fire, the writer has had all the discomforts impressed upon him many times. As a rule, the boys are enthusiastic, and so are the men, and the enthusiasm is most often displayed by the size of the fire; the bigger the fire the greater the delight of the boys and the more difficult the position of the orator or Master of Ceremonies. All this may be overcome, however, if in place of a circle the council grounds are laid out in an oval or an ellipse, and the fire-place located near one end of the ellipse (Fig. 371).

How to Describe an Ellipse

After you have decided upon the size of your council grounds, drive two stakes A and B (Figs. 363 and 365) firmly into the ground; then take a cord, clothesline, or some kind of twine (Fig. 362), and tie the ends together, thus forming a loop (Fig. 363); put the loop over the two stakes A and B; next make a marker stake C (Fig. 366), and with it draw the slack of the line taut as in Fig. 364. The ellipse is marked out as in Fig. 365. This is done by taking firm hold of the top of the stake and using care to keep the line taut while the marker walks around the ground scratching the earth with the point of the marking stick, and allowing the cord to slip smoothly across the stick while the marking is being done (Fig. 364).

WHAT IS AN ELLIPSE?

An ellipse might be called a flattened circle. If you take a tin can and press the two sides of the open end of it inwards, it will form an ellipse. The dictionary says that an ellipse is a conic which does not extend to infinity and whose intersections with the line of infinity are imaginary. Now that is a very lucid explanation! I hope you understand it, it is so simple, but it is just like a dictionary to say such terrible things about a harmless ellipse. To tell the truth, I thought I knew all about an ellipse until I read this explanation; but never mind, we know what it looks like and if we do not know what it is, we do know that there are a lot of things besides ellipses that do not extend to infinity, and we also know that an ellipse is a practical form for a council fire in spite of the hard names the dictionary calls it. This oval is really shaped like the body of a theatre and it gives the audience a chance to see what is doing on the stage, and the people on the stage a chance to see and address the audience.

HOW TO DIVIDE THE COUNCIL FIRE GROUND

This infinity talk has suggested to us a good idea, so we must thank our highbrow dictionary while we lay our council ground out with the major axis (the longest diameter) extending due north and south, and the minor axis (the shortest diameter) extending due east and west, like any other well regulated council or lodge, and we will put the fire-place near the southern end S (Fig. 371), while around the ellipse we will arrange the seats, which may be of logs or stumps or sections of logs set up on end, as I used in one of my camps, or the seats may be rough plank benches, or they may be ponchos spread upon the ground with the shiny side down to keep the dampness from the audience as it squats tailor-fashion upon the ponchos.

THE FOUR COURTS

Are composed of shacks, such as are shown by Fig. 367. He-le-jah (Fig. 371), being the Court of Knowledge, is the only court having an elevated platform, or pulpit, or speaker's stand (Fig. 368). On each side of each court there should be a torch; Fig. 369 is what we will call the camp meeting torch; Fig. 370 is what we will call the steamboat torch; it must be made by a blacksmith. It is an iron basket supported by iron chains, hung down from an iron band at the top of a staff; the latter is shod with an iron point so that it may be thrust into the ground. These fire baskets I have used with success in one of my camps. But homemade torches are to be preferred (see Fig. 369). A band torch (Fig. 373) may be made of pine, spruce or cedar slivers and used for processions entering the council grounds; this gives a thrilling effect.

In the diagram (Fig. 370), the staff is short, but it should be long enough to place the torch as high above the ground as a chandelier is above the floor at home. Fig. 372 shows the method of piling up the wood for the council fire. The kindling wood is first placed upon the ground ready to light at a moment's notice; over that the heavy wood is piled, as shown in the diagram. This fire should never be lighted with a match; that is terrible bad form. The use of flint and steel or a rubbing stick to make fire is the proper ceremony for such occasions.

Fig. 374 shows how to make a fire box of sticks. This is

an aeroplane view of a fire box, that is, a view from above, looking down upon it. This box should be filled with sand, clay or dirt, upon which the fire is built. Fig. 375 and Fig. 376 show you how to lash the framework together. Fig. 377 shows how to put up the framework. Fig. 369 is the finished torch.

The idea of this torch is to have the light above the heads of the campers. The trouble with a fire upon the ground is that while the flames give light they also hide part of the crowd, and the smoke is always in someone's face. This elevated torch is a brand new idea for this purpose. It will be adopted all over the country and credited to all sorts of sources and people, but you must remember that it was designed for the readers of this book.

If milled lumber is used in building the shacks for the four courts, it should be camouflaged with paint or stain so as to look rustic. It may be roofed with boards and the boards covered with tar paper, or any of the modern roofing materials to be had, but in that case the roof should be camouflaged by laying poles over the top of it, or, if poles are not available, covering the top with sods.

You see the idea is this: we are having a COUNCIL FIRE—not something else— and we want the thing to look wild and rustic because that is part of the game, and if we are compelled to go to the lumberyard for our material, which most of us will have to do, then we must conceal this fact as far as possible by camouflage. In front of the South Court on Fig. 371 is the fire-place made of flat stones set in the earth.

COUNCIL FIRE CEREMONIES

On entering the council grounds always enter from the east, salute Too-le-ze, the white wolf, then go across the

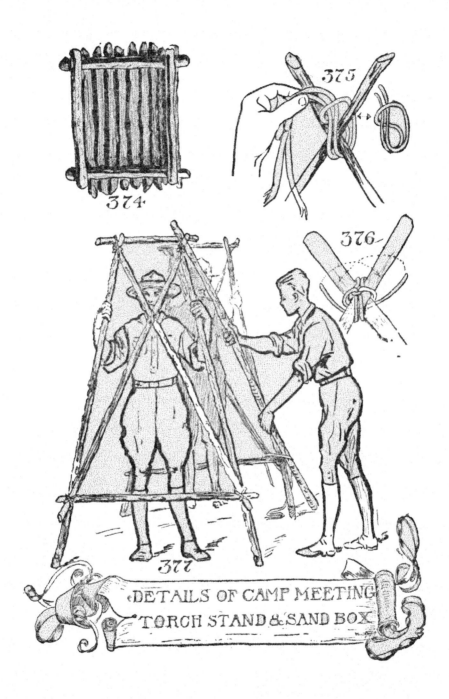

374

375

376

377

DETAILS OF CAMP MEETING
TORCH STAND & SAND BOX

Ghost Walk with the sun to the West Court, and salute Kor-le, the bear; about face and march back to the South Court and salute Too-winks, the badger; then about face and march up and salute He-le-jah, the panther; remain standing at salute until He-le-jah who is the commanding officer, gives you permission to retire, or gives you orders what to do; then go back, always moving along these walks like a soldier, to your seat.

On Sundays the council ground is a splendid place for holding religious services. On such occasions the minister sits in the Court of Knowledge, the North Court on the right-hand side of the presiding officer, and the two torches in the daytime are replaced by flags or banners. The one on the right-hand side of the presiding officer must be Old Glory, the one on the left the flag of the school, the troop or the club to which the council fire belongs.

The center of the council fire may be occupied by a "Liberty Pole," which is the good old American name for the flag pole, from which Old Glory flies. Never forget to respect the colors and greet them with the greatest ceremonial deference, for those colors possess a magic quality; they represent to you everything that is grand, noble and inspiring, and if you have any other kind of thoughts, this country is no place for you. Remember that the council fire is American, and we are proud to be called Americans.

The walk, or path from the east to the west is the Ghost Walk, or the Spirit's Walk; it is the path which Indians believe the spirit takes after leaving the body, an idea which was consciously or unconsciously adopted by our brave boys during the recent war and it explains what they meant when, with bowed heads, they reported that their bunky, pal or friend had "gone West."

The Western Court has the totem animal of the black bear; the color of the court, however, is not black but blue, blue from the blue Pacific; the totem object is a blue mountain.

The walk from the south to the north is the Path of Knowledge; anyone traveling that trail is seeking further knowledge of the benefits of woodcraft, nature and the big outdoors; the totem animal of the North Court is the American panther, cougar or mountain lion; the color of the North Court is yellow or black, the latter representing the long arctic night.

The Southern Court has the badger for its totem animal, and the red mountain for the totem object; red is its totem color.

Thus we have white for the totem color of the east, meaning light, peace and purity; red for the south, meaning violence, disturbance, auction, danger, revolution, love and life. This color is both stimulating and disturbing to man, animal and plant.

Perhaps when we read of the turmoil that is constantly disturbing our southern border, we may think that the Indians had a knowledge of the real meaning of red when they made the totem of the south a red mountain. Red is the ruling color, the king of color, the dominant color, the strong color, and symbolizes the blossoming of plants and is the color of berries and fruit. Red tints the spring leaves and stains the fall leaf. In the spring the thickets and tree trunks are tinged with red; they are blushing, so to speak, as Ruskin says, "in order to show the waiting of love." Red is emphatically a masculine color, a MAN's COLOR.

Blue is a feminine color; it stands for sentimental affections, blue light has a depressing effect and creates nervousness.

Black is the ogre among colors; it devours every other color; sometimes the North Court is black; black stands for war and death, and yet the path to the north is the path of knowledge. It may be that some of the Indians used black for the north because they may have noted that climate affects the color of birds and animals. According to Frank Chapman, the famous ornithologist at the Museum of Natural History in New York, the animals of the humid climate of the northwest are especially dark in color.

If you use yellow for the north color, yellow means laughter and mirth. Notwithstanding the fact that we use yellow as a sign for contagious disease, women suffragists and cowardice, a yellow light makes a gathering cheerful and merry; so in approaching the North Court you may sing.

The Indian names for the four courts are Too-le-ze, the east, for the south Too-winks, for the west Kor-le, and for the north Kon-win. He-le-jah is the Indian name for the panther or mountain lion that guards the north mountain.

Now then you have the symbolism; in other words, know what these things stand for, and that will give a meaning to your ceremony around the council fire. Since red means life and black means death, possibly the Indians have placed a deep significance on the path from the Red Court to the Black Court, from life to death! when they call it the Path of Knowledge. At any rate, we will take it as we find it and adapt ourselves to the suggestions these meanings give us.

We will claim that colors are the spirits, fairies or what not who govern the council fire. Wit-tab-bah is the name of the fire itself or the fire-place. When the fire is built, placed near the Southern or Red Court, it gives the chief, the captain, the superintendent, or the scoutmaster, who occupies the North Court, a space in front of him big enough to accommodate his audience. The real way to illuminate, or light up, the council grounds is by having

Torch Fires

Erected at each of the four courts. These fire torches at the four courts, if kept replenished with dry wood, will light up the council grounds and give a most picturesque and wild appearance, and at the same time will not interfere with the ceremonies nor will they scorch the back or face of the speaker. Wit-tab-bah may be used on occasions when the crowd is not large.

No council fire anywhere within the borders of the United States should open without the pledge to the American flag, and the reciting in unison by all present of the American creed. (See page 268.)

The council should close with the singing of "America." Especially should these ceremonies be gone through with when the assembly is composed of many young people, because what George Washington said in his farewell address is as true to-day as it was a hundred years ago.

"Against the insidious wiles of foreign influences I conjure you to believe me, fellow citizens, the jealousy of a free people ought to be constantly awake, since history and experience prove that foreign influence is one of the most powerful foes of republican government."

There is no reason why we should not have a lot of fun at the council fires, and at times it may even be riotous fun, but always American fun, and the patriotic spirit should never for a moment be forgotten, nor yet the poetic spirit which links us up in bonds of sympathy with all created things so that we may, with seriousness, recite the

INDIAN INVOCATION

O Great Mystery, we beseech thee,
That we may walk reverently
Beneath Lah-pah our brothers, the trees.
That we may step lightly
On Kis-so our kinsmen, the grasses.
That we may walk lovingly
Over Loo-poo-oi-yes our brothers, the rocks.
That we may rest trustfully
Where the O-lel-le bird sings—
Beside Ho-ha-oe, the talking waters.

or this,

Weave for us, O Great Mystery,
A bright blanket of wisdom;
Make the warp the color of Father Sky,
Let He-koo-las, the sun-woman,
Lend her bright hair for the weft,
And mingle with it the red and gold threads of evening.
O Great Mystery; O Mother Earth! O Father Sky!
We, your children, love the things you love;
Therefore, let the border of our blanket
Be bending Ku-yet-tah, the rainbow,
And the fringe be glittering Nuk-kah, the slashing rain.

or with abandon we may sing, or chant the song of the elves,

*Oh, we are the fays, oh, we are the elves,
Who, laughing at everything, laugh at ourselves.
If Fortune's wheel is broke,
Why, we can put a spoke in it.
Misfortune hits no stroke,
But we can put a joke in it.
The owl can do our thinking,
As he sits awinking, blinking.
We act from intuition,
Fun and mischief is our mission;
Solemn duty, we have none of it,
What we do is for the fun of it;
Fun is none too light to prize,
Thought is naught but fancy's flight.
Folly's jolly, wit is wise,
Laughter after all is right.

*From unpublished verses by Captain Harry Beard.

CHAPTER XIV

RITUAL OF THE COUNCIL FIRE

PROGRAM OF A COUNCIL FIRE

INVOCATION

THE PLEDGE AND CREED OF ALL AMERICANS

APPEAL

CHAPTER XIV

RITUAL OF THE COUNCIL FIRE

THE ceremonies of the Council Fire may be conducted with the accompaniment of pageantry to any extent desirable. At the Council Fire of the Dan Beard Outdoor School, the officers dress in costume; not masquerade costumes but the real ones. THE MAN OF THE NORTH, who attends to the Northern Lights, is garbed in the blanket clothes of a northern lumberman and carries an axe. THE MAN OF THE EAST, who attends the fire where the sun maidens dwell, may be arrayed in the clothes of one of our Pilgrim fathers. THE MAN OF THE WEST, who attends the fire of the Blue Mountain, is decked in the fringed buckskin clothes of the trapper, plainsman, or mountaineer. THE MAN OF THE SOUTH, who guards the fire of the Red Mountain, is dressed in the picturesque costume of a Mexican with a high-crowned sombrero. The seats of the different courts are draped with the colors of the courts.

PROGRAM OF A COUNCIL FIRE

The guests enter and take their seats, then the Herald enters dressed in the costume of a scout, a frontiersman, or a medicine man, according to the plan of the particular Council Fire. The Herald faces the north from his stand in the center of the council ground and blows assembly call, or a blast on a cow's horn, then wheels about and faces the east, then the south and then the west, and at each he blows assembly. With the last notes and the last call the Scouts, Woodcrafters, Pioneers or students enter the circle, marching single-file around until the circle is complete, and they stand opposite where they are to sit. The Herald now blows a fan-

267

fare and the officers march into the council ground with the colors and the color guard. The officers group themselves around their Chief, the Scout Executive, the Scout Commissioner, the Headmaster or the man in authority at the North Court.

The Leader, or head officer, steps forward and throwing both hands up in a gesture of appeal, in which he is imitated by the assembly, he repeats:

> Weave for us, O Great Mystery, etc. (as already given).

Then he cries:

> Four Winds of the Earth, we have saluted you!
> Wind of the North, from whence come our snow and ice,
> Wind of the East, from whence come our clouds and rains,
> Wind of the West, from whence comes our sunshine,
> Wind of the South, from whence comes our warmth,
> Send us your men to guard the mystic fires.

The Men of the North, East, West and South, now step in front of the Chief, and he directs them to

> See that the mystic fires are blazing.

The fires, having already been carefully prepared, are now lighted by the fire-keepers under the direction of the men of the Four Winds, and the latter return and report to the Chief in the following manner:

Chief....Man of the North, you whose mighty axe bites to the heart of the pine,
Are the mystic Northern Lights burning at Kon-win?
Is He-le-jah, the Mountain-lion, on guard on the yellow mountain of the North?
Man of the North....Chief, the Medicine fire has been lighted, the Mountain-lion is guarding the yellow mountain of the North,
All is well.

Chief....Man of the East, is the Medicine Fire at Too-le-ze blazing?

Is the White Wolf on guard at the White Mountain, where the sun-maidens dwell?

Man of the East....Chief, Too-le-ze blazes in the East, the White Wolf is on guard. Wah-tab-bah, the robin, shields the fire,

All is well.

Chief....Man of the West, man of the plains and mountains, does the mystic fire at Kor-le blaze?

Is the Black Bear guarding the Blue Mountain, where the sun sets?

Man of the West....Chief, Kor-le is ablaze, the Black Bear's growls may be heard in the torrent that guards the Blue Mountain.

All is well.

Chief....Man of the South, how blazes the fire at Too-winks?

Has the Red Badger come from its burrow to stand guard on the Red Mountain?

Man of the South....Chief, Too-winks flames to the sky. The Red Badger is on guard.

All is well.

The Color Guard now enters, marches up to in front of the officers and all stand at salute. The Color Guard with colors about faces and the guests and all present recite in unison:

THE PLEDGE AND CREED OF ALL AMERICANS

"I believe in the people of the United States, I believe in the United States form of government, I believe in the preamble of the Declaration of Independence, I believe that all men are created equal, that they are endowed by their Creator with certain inalienable rights, among which are Life, Liberty, and the pursuit of Happiness.

"I believe in our Government of the People, by the People and for the People, a government whose just powers are derived from the consent of the governed, a Sovereign Nation of many Sovereign States, a Democracy in a Republic, a perfect Union, one and inseparable.

"A Union which will live because of the vital principles of

Freedom, Equality, Justice, Humanity and Kindness which it contains, and for which American Patriots have willingly sacrificed their lives and fortunes.

"I therefore believe that in order to respect my own manhood I must love my country, support its Constitution and obey its Laws; also that I must respect its Flag, and defend it against all enemies."

After which may come the Scout oath, Pioneer oath or Camp-fire oath, as the case may be. Then the command is given to "spread ponchos," followed by the command "squat!" when all the Scouts, Woodcrafters, Pioneers, or students squat tailor-fashion upon their ponchos, and the guests seat themselves on the benches which have been provided for them.

Following this comes the address by the speakers, the entertainments and exhibitions of woodcraft, scoutcraft, or handicraft, the games, and other entertainment; then follows the awarding of honors. After which all stand to sing "America." Then the Chief or Leader steps forward and repeats the following

APPEAL

O Great Mystery, we beseech thee (as previously given) and ends up with the benediction, in which he uses the Indian phraseology:

"May the Great Mystery put sunshine in all your hearts. Good-night."

362 17

CPSIA information can be obtained
at www.ICGtesting.com
Printed in the USA
LVOW13s2151310718
585463LV00017BA/699/P